Soldiering with
the 'Division'

Soldiering with the 'Division'

The Military Experiences
of an Infantryman of the
43rd Regiment During
the Napoleonic Wars

Thomas Garrety

LEONAUR

Soldiering with the 'Division': the Military Experiences of an Infantryman of the 43rd Regiment During the Napoleonic Wars
by Thomas Garrety

Published by Leonaur Ltd

This book has been adapted by the Leonaur editors from the 1835 volume:
Memoirs of a Sergeant Late in the Forty-third Light Infantry Regiment, Previously to and During the Peninsular War: Including an Account of His Conversion from Popery to the Protestant Religion

Text in this form copyright © 2007 Leonaur Ltd

ISBN: 978-1-84677-406-5 (hardcover)
ISBN: 978-1-84677-405-8 (softcover)

http://www.leonaur.com

Publisher's Note

Contents

Publisher's Note

It would, perhaps, be inaccurate to assert that this book was originally titled *Memoirs of a Sergeant Late in the Forty-third Light Infantry Regiment, Previously to and During the Peninsular War: Including an Account of His Conversion from Popery to the Protestant Religion*, although it is that book, certainly, from which the book you are now holding has been derived.

Whilst every first-hand account of the Napoleonic Wars is both valuable and worthy of being made available to modern readers, it must be acknowledged that this soldier's tale, in its original form, would be likely to tax all but the hardiest students of the era. Although the book was originally published as by 'Anonymous', it's author has now been identified, by Eileen Hathaway, as Thomas Benjamin Garrety.

Garrety was a man of strong religious convictions who found it necessary to intermix rambling allusions to his faith and diatribes on doctrinal matters with an interesting account of his Peninsular War experiences. Like converts throughout history, after his conversion to the Protestant take on Christianity, Garrety turned rabidly against the faith he had once espoused—Roman Catholicism. He believed that his readers would be interested in his anti-Catholic views and, after relating his military experiences, he concluded his book with a lengthy dissertation on matters of faith and theology.

Whilst the Leonaur editors have no problems with works

of a theological nature, we do believe that the content of books is best confined to a single central subject—particularly when readers are likely to be drawn to whatever that central subject is. Thus, a book that purports to be about military life in the British army at the time of Napoleon is, in our view, best confined to that one topic.

For these reasons we have come to the conclusion that Garrety's passages about matters of faith and theology are, unless directly relevant to his military experiences, best excised from our edition of what is—instead—intended to be a military memoir. We believe that although this has reduced the length of the book in terms of total word count it has immeasurably sharpened its focus.

Garrety's literary style—in keeping with that of many of his contemporaries—meant that the reader was required to glean what information there was from a small number of chapters, and interminably long paragraphs that were often spread over many pages. The Leonaur editors have adjusted Garrety's text to create a book with more chapters and shorter paragraphs; by doing this we hope his story will be both more accessible and more interesting for modern readers.

The Leonaur Editors

CHAPTER 1

A Troubled Land

I have the advantage of being an Irishman. My parents had also the felicity of first seeing the light of day as it shone upon the soil of the land which for ages has seemed to possess such passing interest in the eyes of Britain. Their family consisted of six children: four boys, and two girls. I was the youngest of the whole, and, for reasons I do not profess to comprehend, was a special favourite. I was named Thomas; which, interpreted by parental love, was converted into Benjamin, with a double portion of all that substance so scanty as theirs could supply.

I was born in the small towns land of Enneham, King's County, in the province of Leinster, about the year 1790. The exact period I cannot specify; as at that time and place, and in consequence of the culpable negligence generally prevalent in parochial registration, very little thought or care was shown in recording such events.

Those were the days of intestine broil and vengeance. The seeds of rebellion, which had been sown with an unsparing and remorseless hand, were just ready to produce their baneful first-fruit. Such was the jeopardy in which Protestants especially were placed, that no one who beheld the morning sun arise, could safely calculate upon seeing it go down. "Domestic-fury, and fierce civil strife," kindled and mainly maintained by Papal cupidity and violence, raged through the fairest portions of the country. No one had courage to trust his neighbours; for no one could tell who was worthy of trust. Mutual confidence, based upon moral principle, which alone can cement society, was blotted from the list of social virtues. Not many dared depend even upon former friends. The ties of relationship, and those arising from nearness of kin, were frequently forgotten. Natural affection, usually invincible, was unheeded; and under cover of night, or even in open day, the unwary traveller became frequently a prey to instantaneous death from the bullet of some skulking assassin, concealed behind the road-side bush or brake.

My parents, I regret to state, were Roman Catholics. They knew no better; for no other teaching had reached their minds. Their membership with that fallen community was their misfortune rather than their fault. 1 believe the profession they made was sincere; and that, though mingled with the dross of Popish superstition, they were possessors of at least some few grains of sterling piety. My mother, in particular, was remarkably constant and fervid in her devotions; and the earnest manner in which her beads were counted, though I could never detect the meritorious points of calculation, is to be numbered among the earliest and most powerful impressions I ever received. My father had for several years acted as steward to Archibald Nevens, Esq., a gentleman who, at that time, was the owner of considerable estates in the vicinity of Portarlington. Ours was a happy family. My father, though a plain man, was excelled by few in attachment to his wife and children. "Hope springs eternal in the human breast;" and we flattered ourselves that futurity offered to our notice lengthened years of comfort. But we soon found that our hold on earthly happiness was fragile as the spider's thread. My father was taken ill and died. Even now the procession of his funeral is pictured on my memory.

The gentleman already named as my father's employer had fallen upon evil days. His property passed into other hands; and as the purchaser knew nothing of our family, no one cared for the widow and her orphan charge. A house with every needful convenience had been built for us by the original proprietor. This we were abruptly ordered to quit. Another king had arisen, who knew not Joseph or his father's house. We went away, weeping at every step. I saw my mother's tears, and to this day her low wailing strikes my ear. But though destitute, we were not forsaken; though in straits, we did not perish; and by the blessing of Almighty Providence upon the well-directed industry of my mother and my elder brothers, we were sustained with food convenient.

The desolate condition of the moneyless and unprotected widow was aggravated in no common degree by the political commotion already adverted to. Persons unacquainted with the approaching terrors of that era may imagine that an obscure and uninfluential family, like ours, had little to apprehend; that our poverty was protection enough; and that those who had nothing to lose had nothing to fear. Not so. The conflict then impending arose from the dark designs of men "cursed with a heart unknowing how to yield," and who were bent on havoc and rapine. Personal robbery might not be planned, but many were ready for that and a great deal more. Heresy and sedition were closely in league; the emissaries of each were in ceaseless motion; and the ultimate design was, to burst forth from the unsuspecting places of mischief, suddenly, and wide wasting as the simoom of the desert, and sweep with indiscriminating ire, from the abodes of their peaceful countrymen, every vestige of existing government, and every temple devoted to the Reformed religion, as by law and right reason established. Perfect secrecy on the part of the rebels was happily unattainable.

Every now and then circumstances and facts transpired, the tendency of which could not be mistaken. Hair-brained but hot-headed men became the self-elected orators of secluded nocturnal assemblies. Liberty and equality, and reason versus religion, neat as imported from the French Directory at Paris, was the order of the day. Uproarious vociferation took the place of argument; and though the majority of these Hibernian gentry were as ignorant of jurisprudence as the more modern destructionist, nothing less than the dismemberment of the British empire, and the establishment of a republic, formed probably on the model of citizen Robespierre, would suit their purpose. All this was designed, and most of it was divulged. Experience has shown, that where numerous and unequally gifted agencies are employed, let the pursuit be good or evil, entire privacy is next to impossible. The parties may promise to be silent, or may bind themselves to be so by oath; but concealed know ledge is a treasure, of which the custody is to some communicative souls impracticable. They find them selves in the possession of a secret; it struggles to break away; but they remember their vow, and in order to hold it fast, they get a friend or two to help them.

The sons of Irish misrule assumed several names: there were *white-boys*, and *steel-boys*; *oak-boys*, and *right-boys*. Distinctions are, however, needless,—they were all bad boys; and at length the entire series were drawn into the wild and powerful vortex of United Irishmen; it being understood that this body consisted chiefly of persons professing the Roman Catholic religion.

The storm at length came down, and the consequences were awful. Although not quite nine years of age when our neighbourhood rang with war's alarms, the scenes I was then compelled to witness cannot be forgotten. I distinctly remember the transactions of an eventful day which took place in a small town near my mother's residence. The rebels had taken possession of the place, and had murdered a magistrate who attempted to oppose them. At that crisis a squadron of dragoons, stationed at Tullamore, received orders to march and endeavour to dislodge them. The cavalry rode into the

main street with great gallantry, but were received by a tremendous fire of musketry from the windows of the houses
on each side; so that, after sustaining a considerable loss, they
were compelled to retreat. Several of the soldiers were killed;
and a number of wounded men were afterwards conveyed
on cars from the place of action to the military hospital.

My poor mother was in the midst of these dangers; and
I well remember that she experienced great rudeness from
the ruffian rabble. That night we were afraid of entering
into any house, lest we should attract the notice of the
rebels, who were now flushed into insolence and inebriety by their recent victory: we therefore crept behind the
foliage of some low trees, and passed the night in the open
air. Our next precaution was to protect the little remaining
household furniture from pillage. To effect this, we buried
the most valuable articles in the earth, as nothing above
ground appeared to offer the least protection. The property
thus secreted was saved; but on raising it subsequently, almost every thing was spoiled by the dampness of the soil in
which it had been embedded.

One of my neighbours, John Tinkler, was singled out by
these barbarians as a victim. He was a man of singular benevolence, and held in general esteem by the surrounding
inhabitants but he was a Protestant, and that had long been
placed at the head of the list of unpardonable crimes. The
house of this worthy man, whom I well knew, was beset by
a horde of armed ruffians, who commenced an immediate
attack. Tinkler, in the midst of his family, consisting of a wife
and seven or eight children, though surprised, determined
to defend himself to the last extremity. He fought desper-
ately, though oppressed by numbers, until one of the villains posted outside the house, and guided by the sound of
his voice, deliberately levelled his piece and fired. The bullet
passed through the door, and struck Tinkler, who fell dead
just within the threshold, valiantly defending his home and

property; and I regret to add, that the widow and her helpless charge, ejected by some means from the farm and land, were obliged to seek shelter elsewhere.

These were but the beginning of sorrows. The spirit of ruinous anarchy spread far and wide. It was particularly observed, that the Roman Catholics were very much devoted to their chapels. Mass was celebrated every day throughout most parts of the country; whereas, formerly, it was chiefly observed only on the Sabbath-day. The chapel of Ballycanoe was attended by a very numerous congregation at both morning and evening prayers. Michael Murphy was officiating Priest of that parish; a young man, strongly made, and of a dark complexion, who had been a few years resident in the place, and not long in holy orders. This person was master of profound dissimulation, and contrived to throw around himself the garb of saintly innocence at the very moment in which he was preparing to smite with the sword. This military saint actually took the oath of allegiance, in which he expressly declared himself ready to "be true and faithful to His Majesty, King George the Third, and to the succession of his family to the throne; and that he would prevent tumult and disorder by every means within his reach, and give up all sorts of arms in his possession."

"All the above," quoth Michael," I swear, so help me God, and my Redeemer!"

Meantime, in the immediate vicinity and all around the residence of his Reverence, timber was missing out of the gentlemen's nurseries. It was observed that the woods and shrubberies were gleaned of such materials as would suit for the construction of offensive weapons. In fact, this genuine sample of Popish fidelity, who, had he lived, ought to have been rewarded with at least a Cardinal's hat,—this pretended pattern of all that is good and praiseworthy; went his way from the altar, put down the Testament on which, after the perpetration of his delusive affidavit, his lips had been pressed, and straightway began to exemplify the inviolability of his oath to existing government, by the manufacture of pike-handles, and granting absolution to those who helped him.

Without going into the history of the Irish Rebellion, which is foreign from my present purpose, the fact is sufficiently evident, that the whole of that sanguinary struggle from first to last may be ascribed to the crafty domination of the Roman Catholic Clergy. It is not a little singular, that three of the most daring military leaders, those I mean who were principally signalized in the wholesale butchery of their Protestant fellow-subjects, were Priests in that persecuting Church.

One of these, named Roche, assumed the power of working miracles. Indeed, each of them, as occasion required, did a little business in that line. Roche declared, that in battle his person was invulnerable; that no shot could hit or hurt him; and having picked up several bullets after an engagement at Ross, he assured his dupes that he caught them in his hand during the fight. The wily Ecclesiastic, true worshipper as he was at the shrine of Mammon, conceived the idea of turning the thing to good account, by the alternate practice of hypocrisy and theft, for either of which his hand was ready. He succeeded; and I hardly know which to admire most, the consummate impudence of the holy father, or the folly of his disciples. Roche procured slips of paper, each of which he termed a "Protection, or Gospel." In the centre was a figure of the Cross, with an inscription underneath, stating:

In the name of God and of the blessed Virgin, no gun, pistol, sword, or any other offensive weapon can hurt or otherwise injure the person who has this paper in his possession; and it is earnestly recommended to all women to carry it, as it will be found an infallible preservation against the fatality of child-bed.

Anxious to secure customers in every rank, the price of these tickets to the better sort of people was half-a-crown. As the poor might haggle at parting with a coin so large, the vendor discreetly condescended to open a retail trade at six-pence each. The circulation of this trumpery, the value of which was equal to every other product of the Catholic Church, was immense; customers were to be computed by thousands.

Friar Murphy has already been noticed. His career, as has been related, commenced with daring perjury; and as the progress and end of such a man may be instructive, he shall have a parting glance. Like his iniquitous associate, he was disposed to do the wonderful. His campaign, however, with those of many other villains, was soon over. Bloody and deceitful men do not live out half their days. It was at the battle of Arklow, in 1798, that Commander Murphy determined by a decisive movement to blast the hopes of the Protestant cause.

On the morning of the 9th of June, the rebel army was observed, amounting to 34,000 men, with three pieces of artillery, advancing on the town. Had this formidable force arrived only two days earlier, it would in all probability have captured the place; but, providentially, reinforcements bad been procured from Dublin, so that the garrison amounted in the whole to 1500 men, under the command of Major General Needham. Arklow, considered as a military position, presented no points susceptible of advantageous defence, and was altogether open and unprotected. About two o'clock pm. advice was received that the enemy was approaching: this was so little credited that the garrison, which had been ordered under arms, was just going to be dismissed, when a dragoon came galloping into the town with intelligence that the rebels were at hand.

The drums instantly beat to arms, the troops flew to their respective stations, and preparations were made to give the enemy a proper reception. Having advanced to the suburbs of the town, the rebels set fire to several buildings, in hope that the smoke would annoy the garrison, and confuse their operations. Just then the wind shifted to the opposite quarter, so that the scheme not only failed, but served to confound their own devices.

The action commenced between a column of the rebels, and a detachment of the Dunbarton fencibles, who were ordered out to line the ditches on each side of the road. When they had exchanged about a dozen rounds, the fencibles received orders to retreat, which was performed, but with a little confusion. On perceiving this movement, the rebels pursued with loud huzzas, and one of their officers, waving his hat, called out, "Come on, my boys! the town is our own."

That was an error. He was suddenly surrounded by the troops, his horse was shot, and himself wounded; on which he fell as though slain. In a little time curiosity constrained him to lift up his head and look about; when he was perceived, and shot dead. The rebels pressed on with obstinacy worthy of a better cause; but on receiving a close fire of musketry and grape-shot, they fell back to some distance.

They then endeavoured to extend their line in order to turn the left flank, but the fire of the Cavan battalion was so severe, that the attempt was abortive. Another column of the rebels tried to gain the lower end of the town by the beach; but here they were repulsed by a desperate charge of cavalry, headed by Colonel Sir Watkin Wynne. They then proceeded in great force to a passage that led to the centre of the town, which was defended only by a Sergeant and twelve privates: this handful of men, however, made good their position, and, as the pass they held was narrow, rendered every effort to dislodge them from it ineffectual. At this critical juncture Priest Murphy appeared, animating his men to renewed acts of outrage: many of these, terror-stricken by the clamour of this clerical warrior, were driven before him to the thickest of the fray.

As no new deception presented itself, he had recourse to the worn-out pretension of working miracles, He declared, like brother Roche, that he could catch the bullets, or ward them off at pleasure; in proof of which, he advanced at the head of a strong party in order to take a cannon stationed near a barrack. In that moment his bowels were torn out with canister-shot. The rebels, on observing him fall, fled with precipitation, swearing, the Priest himself was down.

On that day a thousand rebels fell. Their retreat, as might be expected, was marked by dreadful excesses: they broke the windows of churches and other places consecrated to divine service. They had an intolerable hatred to Protestant Prayer-books, and tore to pieces all that came within their reach. They carried the leaves of the church Bible on their pikes, shouting, "Behold the French colours!" and, to complete their impiety, they put two Protestants to death in the aisle of a church. In other parts they made saddles of the Bibles, and rode about upon them.

Exposed as my mother and family were to the pelting of the pitiless hurricane, none of us sustained material personal injury.

CHAPTER 2

Enlistment

Meantime I had arrived at the fourteenth year of my age; a period, generally speaking, of no small vanity and self-complacency, and in which many men think themselves qualified, by the dignity of their teens, to shake off the trammels of parental guidance. Among others, I determined to walk alone; but unfortunately I cannot, on reflection, boast of my first step. Among the youths with whom I contracted some acquaintance, was a dissolute lad about my own age; by whose enticement, when only just turned fifteen, I enlisted in the Queen's County militia. Not that my conduct, like his, had been openly immoral; yet he had gained over me an ascendancy I could not resist. Evil communications corrupt good manners; and perhaps the apparent freedom, the frankness and gaiety of an open-hearted soldier's holiday life, had an influence which, though not acknowledged, was really felt. But, O, my mother! for when I became a soldier she was still living. I had in this deed of hardihood well-nigh forgotten her.

But she remembered me; and when I thought thereon, I wept. Never shall I forget her last, her parting look! My elder brother had settled at some distance; and on the eve of my departure to share in unknown danger, had unexpectedly arrived. If bereaved of her children, she was bereaved; and I know she said in her heart, "All these things are against me."

Her farewell was accompanied with a prayer for my future prosperity; and I impute my preservation, under Providence, through life, to the pious lessons and examples of my excellent mother. On leaving her presence on this eventful occasion, I was taken before Captain Fitzmaurice, the officer in command at the recruiting station, and was kindly received. He expressed himself pleased with my look and healthy appearance; made several minute inquiries relative to my family, and at once engaged me as his servant. After serving in the corps about twelve months, I received, principally, I believe, on account of my youth, an honourable discharge, while the regiment was stationed at the Castle-barrack in Limerick, and returned to the quietude of home.

Habits of dissipation may be contracted at pleasure; but when once confirmed by repetition, they are not so easily dismissed. This is especially true in youth; and I soon found that though I had retired beneath the roof of an excellent parent, my disposition to wander wide was still the same. Contentedness of mind I found was a state, not a place. The roll of the spirit-stirring drum, the glittering file of bayonets, with the pomp and circumstance of military parade, not unmingled perhaps with undefined thoughts of ultimate promotion, passed in review before my imagination, in colours vividly charming: resistance was vain. To this alluring panorama was added the consideration that, though only seventeen, I had reached the height of persons required by regimental rule. In fact, on the 6th of April, 1806, I enlisted in the 43rd regiment of the line, and in company with several other recruits proceeded to Cork, where we embarked for Bristol, at which place, after a rough passage, we safely landed; and in a few days reached the town of Ashford, in Kent, where the regiment was quartered.

Events and shifting scenes had crowded one after another, with such rapidity since I left home, that reflection was drowned; but the first night in which I lay down in the barracks, memory began to be busy. I could not help thinking of the peaceful fire-side I had left; and in despite of my most vigorous effort to shake off the intrusion, conscience would not be denied, and the image of my mother, deserted at her utmost need, and pinched perhaps by want, was a source of great uneasiness. But having passed the Rubicon, retreat I knew was out of the question.

Independently of the conflict within, my situation in the barrack was not adapted to afford much present consolation. The sleeping-room of which I was an inmate was an oblong building of unusually large dimensions, and was occupied by three companies, of an hundred men each. They were chiefly volunteers, and of course young soldiers. Many were Irish, many more were English, several Welshmen were intermingled, and a few Scotchmen came in to complete the whole. Most of these, and that was the only point of general resemblance, had indulged in excessive drinking. Some were uproariously merry; on others the effect was directly the reverse; and nothing less than a fight, it mattered not with whom, would satisfy.

Meantime as they were unable to abuse each other in language mutually intelligible, exclamations profanely jocular, or absurdly rancorous, rang through the building; altogether the coalition of discordant verbiage was such as to beggar all description, and can be likened to nothing of which I ever heard or read, except the confusion on the plains of Babel. Never will the occurrence of that night be effaced from my mind. Surely, thought I, hell from beneath is moved to engulf us all. These disorderly proceedings, thank God, were of short continuance. In a few weeks we marched to more convenient quarters, a few miles distant. The salutary restraints of discreetly managed discipline spake chaos into order, and my situation became comparatively comfortable.

How it has happened I know not, but through all the changes of my life, and they have been neither few or tri-

21

fling, I never lacked a friend. One of the first of these has been alluded to; and another belonged to the battalion to which I found myself attached, and, though no relative of mine, was of the same name. He was exceedingly kind on numerous occasions; and it will be readily believed, that the smallest act of civility in favour of a mere novice, at the commencement of his military life, was valuable. The drill of the regiment was severe; but I passed muster without difficulty, and had, in addition, the good fortune, to attract the notice of our Colonel, a fine old Scotchman; and the first time I mounted guard I was selected by the Adjutant as his Orderly. This preference, as I had never seen actual service, was perhaps to be imputed to neatness of dress, and, the condition of my arms and accoutrements, in which, though only a private, I saw it my duty to be particular; added to this, I was remarkable for flexibility of limb and muscular power, thoroughly understood the use of my weapons, and, unless flattered, had the advantage of a good figure.

That was a period of uncommon vigilance throughout the British army, especially with regard to the corps stationed along the shores of Kent. On the opposite side, and almost within sight, numerous and well-disciplined masses of troops had for some time been encamped under the personal inspection, it was said, of Napoleon, who entertained the vain-glorious project of conquering Britain.

The harbour of Boulogne contained a numerous and well-appointed flotilla, in which were to embark the long-expected invading force. In the opinion of the best judges, the attempt, even with favouring wind and tide, would have failed. Had the navigation of the high seas by the medium of steam been understood and applied at that time, a naval engagement, in the view of perhaps both countries, might have recalled the fury of the ancient Armada, and would probably have been fought upon principles of destructive tendency, till then untried. Not that the result need be doubted.

Had it been possible for a few gun-boats or flat-bottomed craft to elude the vigilance of an English fleet, and shoot a little rubbish upon our borders, no material injury could have arisen. Not a foreigner would have survived to tell the tale of his rashness. I know the spirit of the British army both at home and abroad, and can safely aver, that they would have given an excellent account of the intruders, or perished in repelling them. The experiment was not to be made: Providence ordered that these aggressive movements should begin and end in gasconade. Some good man has said, that the Almighty places the hedge of his providence around the abode of his people, and the hedge of his grace around their souls. My opinion is, that these are the defences within which we are entrenched; and that while we keep within the guarded circle, every foe, whether secret or open, will be kept at bay.

In June, 1807, our regiment, which numbered a thousand effective men, was called into actual service; and I soon had an opportunity of observing the difference between the good-humoured rencontres of a holiday review, and the tug and strife of desperate conflict.

This country, as is well remembered by thousands, stood, at the beginning of the present century, nearly, if not quite, alone against the colossal influence of continental despotism. The Emperor of the French, then at the zenith of power and ambition, seemed determined to compass the globe in exertions to ruin the commerce and prosperity of England. Its welfare was an intolerable worm at the root of all his enjoyment; and among other plans in which it gratified his soul to revel, was that of forming a confederacy among the northern powers of Europe, for the purpose of excluding the vessels of this country from the navigation of the Germanic waters, and bringing against it the concentrated strength of hostile navies.

In this alliance it was supposed that Denmark had largely shared; and as Lord Nelson had already shown that the passage of the Sound was not so impregnable as had been thought, the British Ministry resolved to send an expedition, consisting both of land and sea forces, for the purpose of capturing Copenhagen, together with the fleet in that harbour. This singular determination was defended in Parliament, not by charging the Danes with hostile intentions, but by urging their inability to resist the increasing power of France. In the opinion, however, of several creditable writers on jurisprudence and the laws of nations, the measure is to be deplored, not only because it is dishonourable in itself, but calculated to render our name odious in a country where we should otherwise have found cordial allies. There are some, observes an Apostle, that say, "Let us do evil, that good may come." Such was the case apparently here, and the abettors of the act place themselves within the malediction that followed.

The argument of the British Cabinet was— It is possible that our antagonists, who want valuable ships, may seize the Danish navy: this is the more likely because effectual resistance cannot be offered: to remedy this awful breach of justice, in respect of a harmless neutral power, we will save all farther trouble, by taking possession of the property ourselves. An illustration of three lines exhibits the unfairness of the transaction:— A well-armed freebooter pounces upon his peaceable neighbour, ransacks his habitation, breaks open his coffers, abstracts the property, seriously wounds the sufferer in the scuffle, and marches off with the spoil: the burglar then justifies the act, because he has heard, that unless he make haste, an acquaintance of his, as great a thief as himself, but a far inferior pirate, with whom he has quarrelled, has thought of doing the very same thing.

The Government of this country supported itself on the occasion by several reasons. They urged that the Danish fleet and stores, but for the proposed interposition, must fall into the hands of Bonaparte, who wanted exactly that kind of force to act against his formidable foe; that Denmark was totally unable to prevent the seizure of her ships; that there was ground to believe that in order to conciliate the esteem of the French ruler, she would willingly yield to his desire; that in either case, the result would be equally unfavourable to this country, inasmuch as the well-appointed fleet of our northern neighbours would supply our inveterate enemy with the means of annoyance in which his greatest deficiency was apparent; and that the rigid inexorable law of necessity and self-preservation not only permitted, but demanded, the previous seizure of the instruments of intended war. But the causes of hostility between nations involve considerations concerning which a soldier is seldom called upon to trouble himself. Generally speaking, he has little right to meddle or make concerning them. While others reason, he is to obey orders, to fight and fear not; the questions he asks for conscience sake being few and far between.

CHAPTER 3

The Danish Campaign

It was on the morning of a delightful day, that we broke up our quarters at Hythe, on our route to the place of embarkation. The scene was novel, and to myself, who witnessed it for the first time, highly impressive. We breakfasted on the heights of Dover, and in the course of the day marched to Deal. On the following morning, we proceeded to Ramsgate. Boats for our conveyance to the transports then at anchor in the Downs were moored off the pier-head, and in a short time I found myself on board the *Sally*, formerly of Shields, which had been engaged by Government, and fitted up for the reception of troops.

The embarkation was effected in August, 1807; and I know not that any event, either before or since, connected with the casualties and privations of military life, ever struck my mind with greater force than that to which I now refer. I allude principally to the strength of affection evinced by the soldiers' wives and children, many of whom resolutely followed in the line of our march, and whom it was impossible to shake off, though permitted to follow to the edge of the water. Indeed many were not con tent with that: several women insisted on going with their husbands into the boats, and actually did so. "Father," I heard a little child say, "shall I never see you again!" The grief of separation at last was inevitable; and on nearing the ship's side, I saw many an embrace, destined by the fitful chances of war to be the last indulged on earth.

The fleet destined for the north bore away from the Downs with a fine leading breeze. It consisted of forty-two ships of war, twenty-two of which were of the line, several frigates, and a forest of transports, on board of which the forces destined to act on shore were embarked: these amounted to twenty thousand effective men, and were under the command of Lord Cathcart, while Admiral Gambier directed the naval operations.

After a rough passage, we came in sight of the Danish coast about the middle of August; and early on the morning of the 16th of that month, the debarkation of the troops, under cover of several gun-brigs, commenced. We landed at Wisbeck, a small place in the island of Zealand, about eight miles from Copenhagen. Just before leaving the vessel in which I had sailed, I had a narrow escape. The weather being warm and fine, several of the soldiers and sailors took the advantage of bathing, and I made one of the number.

One morning, after having enjoyed this luxury, and just as I was half-dressed, a cry of distress was heard, and on looking over the ship's side, a sailor, evidently unable to swim, was observed, endeavouring to float on the surface of the water by grasping an oar that happened to be within his reach: unfortunately he was unable to retain his hold, and immediately disappeared. The sea was calm, and so remarkably clear, that the spot in which he sank was easily recognised. Not a moment was to be lost; and, being an expert swimmer, I divested myself of the clothing I had put on, and dived after him.

On looking about, I saw the poor fellow faintly struggling near the bottom, among some long sedgy weeds: his head being still uppermost, I seized him with one hand by the hair, and with the other was so far able to swim, as to raise both the man and myself to the surface, when on a sudden he fastened on me with a grasp so deadly, that I was incapable of moving hand or foot; and had I not been able to disengage myself, I must inevitably have perished. The struggle between us was terrific, being myself at that time scarcely seventeen years of age, and he a powerful full-grown man.

At length, by a desperate effort; I escaped from his grasp. Deprived of my buoyancy, he sank like a stone. On account of the length of time I had been under water, my preservation was little less than miraculous; indeed, one of the officers, and several of the crew, who witnessed the transaction, had given me up for lost; when to their surprise, I again emerged, and was safely taken on board. Diligent search was made for the body of the poor man, but without effect: it had, no doubt, drifted with the current far from the place in which the accident occurred, to be found probably no more till the sea shall give up her dead.

After the army had made good its landing, which was effected without opposition, one of the first acts of our commander was to issue a proclamation, in which he announced the object of the expedition, lamented the necessity of the cause of it, and expressed a hope that the Danish fleet, then at anchor in the roads, would be surrendered without bloodshed; at the same time declaring, that if it were not given up, force would be used to secure it; in which event, he argued, the innocent blood unavoidably shed would be chargeable on those who advised resistance to a measure dictated by imperious necessity.

To this specimen of military logic, rendered so conclusive by the force of arms, the Danes deigned no reply. The Government resolved to defend the capital, and thus convince the world, that the country intended to maintain its honour and property against the assailants, whether they came from the Thames or the Seine, and show the fallacy of the reasoning upon which the British Ministry founded the expediency of their present extraordinary measure. Paper contentions and the rivalry of manifestoes were therefore relinquished;

and as neither party chose to recede, negotiation was succeeded by the rude appeal to arms.

On the side of the invaders, the best understanding subsisted between the army and navy, and suitable arrangements were promptly made by the respective commanders for mutual cooperation. Several frigates and gun-boats took advantage of a favourable wind to place themselves in front of the harbour, taking care to secure a position which enabled them to throw shells into the city, while the troops advanced by land: the operations on both elements were conducted with equal vigour and success.

The plan of defence adopted by the Danes was similar to that projected some years previously, in the memorable engagement with Nelson. Strong lines of gun-boats and prams were securely moored for the defence of the harbour flanked at each extremity by the crown Battery, and a Block-House, in which upwards of an hundred pieces of cannon were mounted: this force, which was judiciously planned, offered formidable resistance to the British squadron.

The Danes fired red hot balls, and soon after the commencement of the action several of our ships in advanced positions were compelled to haul off: they, however, shortly resumed their places, and poured an incessant fire on the rafts and armed craft. As it was deemed imperatively needful to put an end to all resistance on the harbour side of the city, batteries were erected on shore by the English forces, who opened a well-directed fire on every vessel in which Danish colours were visible.

Congreve rockets flared through the lurid sky without intermission. One of the Danish vessels blew up with tremendous explosion: the fire of the others gradually abated, and in a few hours all opposition from the flotilla ceased. Meantime the main body of the besieging army pushed on its advanced posts with great vigour: they carried their approaches to within four hundred yards of the ramparts, and forced one of the strongest redoubts, which was turned against the enemy.

Having heard that a considerable body of troops had assembled in order to surprise us, a detachment, consisting of four regiments of British infantry, with a squadron of Hussars, under the command of Sir Arthur Wellesley, was ordered to march against it. We found the Danes fourteen thousand strong, advantageously posted in front of the small town of Kioge.

The attack began on our part with the usual spirit. Some little impression having been made on the enemy's line, the 92nd were ordered to charge: the movement was executed with astonishing celerity; the shock was irresistible, and the Danes, unused perhaps to such personality, fled in all directions: numbers, however, remained lifeless on the battle-field, and many more were taken prisoners, and consigned to the British fleet.

As this was the first action of any importance in which I had been closely engaged, it put my firmness to the test. The regiment in which I served was placed on the right of the British line. The first thing that startled me, was the forceful rebound of a cannon ball that struck the ground within a few paces of the place where I stood: it scattered the earth with violence, but fortunately did no injury; and the impression of danger was soon erased by the heavy and rapid trampling of a cavalry charge made in our favour, and which laid many a brave fellow low. Of those who escaped from the destructive sweep, several sought refuge in a church-yard, where a large body were overtaken and captured.

I recollect meeting with an exhausted Dane, concealed in the side of a ditch: the interview seemed particularly disagreeable to him, and was quite unexpected by myself. I soon put an end to all explanations, by conducting him to head-quarters. But after the battle had ceased, and my spirits became composed, I was subdued beyond all I ever felt before. This emotion was produced by leisurely traversing the scene of action on the following day. There lay the dead, just as they had fallen. They were said to be enemies, but I felt that they and myself were partakers of one common nature. I saw several Danish women, moving with terror among the slain, anxious to discover, and yet afraid to ascertain, who pressed the field.

The day before I was among the foremost of those fearless spirits who dealt out wounds and carnage, careless of danger, and destitute of fear. But when the soul is allowed quietly to look within; when the hurricane of wrath has spent its fierceness, and nothing remains, save the desolation it has produced, views and sensations are strangely transposed. My compassionate musings were, however, exceedingly brief. A soldier's moral meditations seldom take place; and if nature will occasionally assert her right, the hasty tear is brushed away for sterner thoughts and deeds.

There is to be perceived among the Danes an amiable simplicity of manners, coupled with remarkable firmness and bravery in action: this was conspicuous in every conflict. Private emolument, or the protection of property was never suffered to compete with the measures necessary for public defence. Life itself seemed of value only so far as it could contribute to national honour. Gardens, smiling with the choicest fruits, all but ripe, were cheerfully resigned as the site for erecting batteries. Masses of soldiery were quartered in the corn-fields. The furniture of several mansions belonging to the nobility was hastily removed, and the buildings offered to the service of Government, as the exigency of affairs required. The palace of the Crown Prince resembled a barrack more than the residence of royalty. The entire people, of whatever age or rank, emulous only to be distinguished in the defence of home, came simultaneously forward, with the suffrage of their best services. This unflinching devotedness, estimable, whether in friend or foe, was met by corresponding energy on the part of the besiegers, who were persons not to be trifled with.

CHAPTER 4

Copenhagen

Before I report further progress, a few brief notices of the city of Copenhagen may not be uninteresting. It is universally acknowledged to be the best-built capital in the north. Petersburg excels it in superb edifices, but is disfigured by multitudinous wooden houses, and exhibits therefore a striking contrast of pomp and penury. Copenhagen presents a more equable and uniform appearance.

The town is surrounded toward the land with regular ramparts and bastions, a broad ditch full of water, and several outworks. Its circumference is about five miles. The streets are well paved, with a foot-way on each side, but are inconveniently narrow. The greater part of the buildings are of brick, and a few of freestone brought from Germany. The houses of the nobility are in general splendid, and constructed in the Italian style of architecture: the palace, which was erected by Christian VI., is a large pile of building, the front of which is stone, and the wings of brick stuccoed.

Maritime affairs, and the facilities of trade, have also received proper attention. The haven is commonly crowded with merchant ships, and the streets are intersected with broad canals, by which merchandise is brought close to the warehouses that line the quays. The city owes its principal beauty, and healthiness, to a cause similar to that to which the renovation and improvement of London are to be ascribed. A

dreadful fire broke out in Copenhagen, in 1728. Five churches and sixty-seven streets were destroyed; the whole of which,
and many others, have since been rebuilt in modern style.
The new part of the town, raised by the late King, Frederick
V, is extremely beautiful, scarcely inferior to Bath. It consists
of an octagon, containing four uniform and elegant buildings of hewn stone, and of four broad streets leading to it
in opposite directions. Part of Copenhagen, which is called
Christianshafen, is built upon the isle of Amak.

The British Commander, unwilling to injure the city, had
hitherto confined his offensive operations to the adjacent
suburbs. It was, however, notified to the Danes in occupation
as a garrison, that unless the terms proposed for the surrender of the fleet were immediately accepted, an attack might
be expected.

On the 31st of August the platform was raised, and the
mortar batteries were ready for action. General Pieman, the
Governor, having refused to listen to the proposals forwarded, a vigorous fire was opened from the batteries and bomb-
vessels, and in a few hours it was observed that the city was
on fire in several places: the bombardment continued with
little intermission till the evening of the 7th of September.
By that time, extensive injury had ensued, and it became
evident that if the bombardment continued much longer,
the city would be reduced to ashes.

A flag of truce was in this extremity despatched, request-
ing a suspension of hostilities for twenty-four hours, to afford time for proposing terms of capitulation. The reply of
Lord Cathcart was, that nothing of the kind could be entertained, unless grounded on the entire and unconditional
surrender of the Danish fleet.

This was a bitter pill; but necessity, which has often laid
the mighty in the dust, compelled the besieged to take it;
and in the night of the 7th of September, the articles of
capitulation were settled, to be ratified the following morn-

ing. According to these, the British were put into possession of the citadel and dockyards; all the ships of war and naval stores were to be delivered up; a mutual restoration of prisoners was to take place, private property to be respected, and in the space of six weeks the citadel to be restored to the King of Denmark, and the whole island of Zealand to be evacuated by the British army.

In consequence of this capitulation, we were put into possession of sixteen sail of the line, fifteen frigates, six brigs, and twenty-five gun-boats, all of which were nearly ready for sea. A vast abundance of stores of all kinds necessary to equip or build a fleet were found in the arsenals. It was therefore necessary to load all the ships of the line and frigates which were delivered up, with masts, spars, and timber; so that ninety-two transports were employed to bring the property to England.

Whatever may be the opinion respecting the justice or policy of the expedition to Copenhagen, there can be but one relative to the mode in which Lord Cathcart conducted it. While he did all that his duty as an officer required, he was throughout the whole of the operations attentive to the suffering Danes: he levied no contributions; not the slightest military excess was committed; and had it not been that the British army was engaged in bombarding their capital, the Danes might have taken them for friends and allies, instead of hostile troops. Even after the surrender of Copenhagen, we were not quartered in it for some days; the Danish troops remaining in possession of all the gates but that which was connected with the citadel.

No interference took place with respect to the police, or any other internal regulation of the city, and every thing was done to tranquillize the public mind: but all was in vain to reconcile the Danish Government or people to the bombardment of the capital, and the seizure of their fleet in time of peace.

As might have been foreseen, the outrage was deemed intolerable: it is true they were plundered with comparative politeness,—nobody hurt them when their treasures were given up; still that did not alter the character of the transaction: it conferred honour upon the agencies employed, who might, without any special departure from the laws of war, have added fierceness to bravery, and wasted what they did not want. But the national spirit of the Danes was roused to unquenchable indignation; they considered themselves the victims of lawless freebooters, superior to themselves only in brute force, and infinitely inferior in every thing else. Under feelings excited by these galling considerations war was proclaimed between Denmark and Great Britain.

Every one will readily believe, that, notwithstanding the good behaviour of their visitors, the Danes were by no means enamoured with our company, and not a little pleased when preparations were made for departure. We had caused great injury to several of the finest erections in the city; had thrown down the steeple of one of the best churches; had created an entire suspension of commerce for a wearisome season; and having collected as much naval property as we could grasp, and more than we could carry, were getting it on board the captured vessels with as much deliberation and order as if nothing more were in hand than a regular shipment of purchased merchandise. The design of the expedition having been fully executed, the troops were re-embarked towards the end of October.

CHAPTER 5

Back to England

On observing the signal for sailing, the whole of the fleet prepared to weigh, and stand out to sea; and when under sail, the almost interminable line of shipping presented an extensive and magnificent spectacle. The first part of the homeward voyage was performed under favourable circumstances; but on nearing the English coast, the weather, which had been fine, became rough and boisterous. Soon after we came in sight of land, the regiment to which I belonged, for reasons with which I am unacquainted, was shifted from the vessel we had occupied, to the *Sirion*, of seventy-four guns, one of the Danish prizes; and though so near our destined port, we were exposed to danger, greater perhaps than any we had hitherto experienced. There were on board, beside the crew, seven companies of the 43rd, amounting to nearly as many hundred men.

Just at midnight, during a gale of wind, when all were wrapt in security, and the greater part in slumber, the ship struck on a sand-bank. The shock was excessively violent. Alarmed by the concussion, which was attended by an ominous straining of the timbers, an immediate rush was made by the soldiers below to gain the main deck. To prevent this dangerous intrusion, the hatches were secured, and a strong guard appointed to keep them from being forced.

The confusion and contention that prevailed among such

a body of resolute men, cooped up in their berths between decks, and with the consciousness of danger, which they were not even permitted to view, may be conceived, but not easily described. To increase our alarm, the foremast went over with several men in the top, one of whom fell on the shank of an anchor, and was killed. By the mercy of God we were after all preserved.

Several of the most active soldiers, among whom I was one, were eventually ordered to assist the crew, whose exertions were beyond all praise. The damaged rigging and running tackle were all repaired; we contrived, under the direction of the ship's officer, to elevate a jury mast, and exhibit canvass that answered the purpose of a foresail; and though in a shattered condition, we had the happiness, assisted by a favourable breeze, to feel the ship glide over the shoal, and swing into deep water.

On the following day, the sailor who lost his life by falling from the fore-top was committed to the deep. The body was carefully enclosed in a blanket, and placed on an oblong grating, to each end of which two round shot were lashed. The sea-service for the burial of the dead was then performed with great solemnity; immediately after which, the grating was lowered from the ship's side, and, being heavily weighted, sunk with the velocity of a stone.

We landed in safety at Yarmouth, on the first day of December, and marched without loss of time into the barracks, where all traces of our recent perils and exposure to sudden mortality were soon forgotten, or remembered only for amusement.

Having saved a little money, I was soon able to furnish myself with such extra articles of necessity and convenience as appeared desirable to a young man just returned to his native shore, and aiming to appear respectable. But, alas! I regret to state, that my ambition was not limited to things altogether needful. Surrounded by evil examples, I became an easy prey to vicious men and their sinful practices. Prodigal of cash, while it lasted, the earnings of many a watchful, hard-fought day were speedily dispersed.

When war's alarms are heard, the soldier reckons only upon short repose; and after remaining a few weeks on the coast, the regiment to which I belonged was ordered into winter quarters. While stationed there, we bad the misfortune to lose two of our officers, both of whom sank into an untimely grave. One of them fell a victim to the pernicious practice of duelling, and the other was drowned by incautiously venturing beyond his depth while bathing. During the time we remained in the neighbourhood the unceasing kindness of the inhabitants was remarked by us all. In the spring of the ensuing year we were ordered to Colchester, in the vicinity of which several regiments were quartered ready for active service, and expecting daily orders to embark for the Continent. The anticipated directions from London, so impatiently desired, arrived in the autumn of 1808: we were ordered instantly to prepare for foreign service; and never, I verily believe, was an invitation to a feast more readily obeyed. The regiment mustered in full strength, the men were in excellent condition; a brief and hearty farewell was all we could spare for friends at home, and in an incredibly short period we were afloat at Harwich, from whence we sailed to Falmouth to await the arrival of other transports.

CHAPTER 6

To Spain

In the course of a few days, the squadron had assembled, and immediately made sail. We soon found that our destination was Corunna, in the north of Spain. The discovery led to a variety of conjecture, and speculation was busy in marking out the nature of our future service. The general opinion was, that we should not suffer from idleness: eager for the fray, nothing was coveted save a clear stage and no favour; victory was reckoned on as a matter of course, and as to the hardships and disasters of a hostile or contested land, every inch of which was to be fought for, the idea had no existence, or was dismissed as a trifle. Happy ignorance of the future, where prescience itself, unless true wisdom had been added, could only have depressed the mind. I am happy on reflecting that during the whole of our march not a man was missing; no one slinked, and in the future conduct of the 43rd, no one, that I ever heard of, deserted his colours or disgraced his country: but out of the many hundred of gallant fellows that then composed our honourable corps, how few were destined to see their native land again!

Our voyage was remarkably pleasant, and we landed at the desired haven without danger or loss. The harbour of Corunna is spacious and safe, and the town is defended by batteries and guns mounted at all points. The citadel is also strongly fortified, but both are commanded by heights within a short distance. Within the houses of the inhabitants there is little to suit the taste of an Englishman the weather when I was there, though cold and chilly, seldom produced the sociable sight of a cheerful fire within doors; indeed, I never observed so much as a hearth or stove in which to kindle one.

Without in the least entering into political detail connected with the causes and result of the memorable Peninsular campaign, which is not within my present design, it may be enough to state, that the expedition in which I had sailed was planned by the British Government to act in concert with several simultaneous movements in favour of the Spanish Constitutionalists then contending with their French invaders.

Our arrival in October, 1808, proved to be a momentous crisis: a few weeks previously, Bonaparte had entered Spain, and taken the command of the hostile army, with the avowed purpose of driving the English into the sea. He advanced as usual by marches prodigiously rapid, on Madrid, so that at the end of November his advanced guard reached the important pass of Somosierra: this pass was defended by 13,000 Spaniards, with sixteen pieces of cannon. They were attacked by the French under the Duke of Belluna, and after a vigorous resistance entirely defeated.

On the 2nd of December Bonaparte arrived in the vicinity of Madrid, and in three days from that period was master of that capital. Dispirited and overwhelmed as the Spanish generally were by the presence of the hero of Jena and Austerlitz, it was evident they were unable, unless assisted by foreign allies, to resist the advances of such masses of troops as those now within their dominions. British co-operation was therefore sought and obtained. Its value, and the fidelity of the army it employed, had already been proved in Portugal, where, with a force decidedly inferior, the invaders were repulsed at Vimiera, with unusual loss.

As a temporary residence at Corunna, we had been placed in a long uncomfortable building, formerly used as a factory or rope-walk. On the following day marching orders were received, when the entire division was put into motion; and leaving the coast, our route lay through Lugo, Villa Franca, and Benevente. After halting for a short time, we crossed the Esla, and arrived at Sahagan, where we were ordered to remain. The light corps occupied an extensive convent built on each side of a square, in whose immense galleries several thousand infantry were accommodated: a numerous body of monks, with other persons of similar sanctity, notwithstanding our heretical exterior, had also taken refuge under the same roof.

On leaving the convent, we advanced in close order for several miles; when from the superior force of the enemy, it was judged advisable to retreat. A counter-march by sections was ordered, and just be fore midnight we had fallen back upon the line of our former route. Here we were directed to lighten our knapsacks as much as possible, and divest ourselves of every needless encumbrance.

Meantime the advanced guard of Benevente's army had broken up from Tordesillas, and strong detachments of cavalry had been pushed forward to Majorga. On the 26th Lord Paget fell in with one of these parties at the latter place; his Lordship directly ordered Colonel Leigh, with two squadrons of the 10th Hussars, to attack this corps, which had halted on the summit of a steep hill. On approaching the top, where the ground was rugged, the Colonel judiciously reined in to refresh the horses, though exposed to a severe fire. When he had nearly gained the summit and the horses had recovered their breath, he charged boldly, and overthrow the enemy; many of whom were killed and wounded, and above a hundred made prisoners.

The brigade of which our regiment formed part, was under the command of General Crawford. Just before, or nearly at the moment of, our arrival on the banks of the river Esla, the principal part of the British forces, under Sir John Moore, were rapidly passing; the stores were conveyed by Spanish mules. We were in the rear, and the enemy pressed forward with such impetuosity that the chasseurs of the Imperial Guard were frequently in sight, and, unable perhaps to do more, captured some women and baggage. Exposed as we were to the assault of a vigilant and superior foe, not a moment's repose could be obtained; and it has seldom happened that personal courage has been put to a severer test.

Permit me to recite an instance:— John Walton, an Irishman, and Richard Jackson, an Englishman, were posted in a hollow road on the plain beyond the bridge, and at a distance from their piquet. If the enemy approached, one was to fire, run back to the brow of the hill, and give notice if there were many or few; the other was to maintain his ground. A party of cavalry, following a hay-cart, stole up close to these men, and suddenly galloped in, with a view to kill them and surprise the fort. Jackson fired, but was overtaken, and received twelve or fourteen severe wounds in an instant; he came staggering on, notwithstanding his mangled state, and gave the signal. Walton, with equal resolution and more success, defended himself with his bayonet, and wounded several of the assailants, who retreated, leaving him unhurt; but his cap, his knapsack, his belt, and his musket were cut in above twenty places, and his bayonet was bent nearly double, his musket covered with blood, and notched like a saw from the muzzle to the lock. Jackson escaped death in his retreat, and finally recovered of his wounds.

On the 27th, the cavalry being all over the river, preparations were made to destroy the bridge: torrents of rain and snow were descending. The cavalry scouts of the enemy were abroad, and a large party, following the store-wagon, endeavoured to pass the piquet, and gallop down to the bridge.

The design was perceived and defeated. Smart skirmishing was kept up all the day; but the masonry of the bridge was so solid, that midnight had arrived before the arches could be materially injured. We then descended the heights on the left bank, and passing with the greatest silence by single files over planks laid across the broken arches, gained the other side without loss,—an instance of singular preservation, as the night was dark and tempestuous, and the enemy almost within hearing. The mine was almost immediately after sprung with good effect,—I mean the bridge was ruined; while we marched forward to Benevente, where the cavalry and the reserve still remained. Here we re-entered the convent which had given us protection on a former occasion.

During the brief stay made here, we experienced a remarkable escape from imminent danger. The lower corridors of the building were filled with the horses of the cavalry and artillery, so thickly stowed that it was scarcely possible for a single man to pass them, and there was but one entrance. Two officers returning from the bridge, being desirous to find shelter for their men, entered the convent, and with terror perceived that a large window-shutter was on fire. The flame was spreading to the rafter above; in a few moments the straw under the horses would ignite, and six thousand men and animals be involved in inevitable ruin.

One of the officers, (Captain Lloyd, of the 43rd,) a man of great activity, strength, and presence of mind, made a sign to his companions to keep silence, and springing upon the nearest horse, ran along the backs of the others until he reached the flaming shutter, which he tore off its hinges, and threw out of the window; then returning quickly, he awakened some of the soldiers, and cleared the passage without creating any alarm, which in such a case would have been as destructive as the flames. I scarcely need add, that Captain Lloyd was a man of more than ordinary talent.

The town of Benevente, a rich open place, is remarkable

for a small but curious Moorish palace or castle, containing a fine collection of ancient armour, and is situated on an extensive plain, that, extending from the Gallician mountains to the neighbourhood of Burgos, appeared to be boundless. Here the army rested two days; but as little could be done to remove the stores, the greater part was destroyed, of which I was a reluctant eye-witness.

I am sorry to say, that during this sojourn, the fine discipline of our corps, thus far maintained without a flaw, was sadly broken down. Some circumstances may be urged in mitigation of the fault, though, looking at that eventful crisis, nothing can altogether extenuate the excesses into which numbers of the troops descended. Exhausted as they were with privation and fatigue, it is no wonder that they were eager in search of repose and refreshment.

Unfortunately one of the first objects of attention was an extensive range of vaults, in which pipes of wine were deposited. In such haste were the half-famished men to quench their thirst, that shots were fired at the heads of the casks, which sent them in altogether, so that the choice and heady liquor ran in all directions, and was ankle-deep on the pavement; beside which, and this was the most serious part of the calamity at such a moment, the men, regardless of the potent and intoxicating beverage, drank it like water. The result need not be told; and I have often thought it was a special mercy that at such a juncture the services of the men were not required. Had the enemy approached, no one could have averted the fate of the aggressors. Unable either to fight or fly, they must have fallen into hostile hands, in all the disgrace of impotent inebriety.

It has often been to myself a source of satisfaction, that on the occasion referred to I was preserved from the excesses described. Not that I can take credit for possessing at the time any extraordinary measure either of virtuous principle or religious light; yet I was not without a strong sense of duty. The good advices of my mother were frequently up-permost; and many a time, when hard pressed by hunger and perilous service, my mind was supported by a persuasion that my mother was praying for my preservation.

From the temporary mischief alluded to we soon recovered. Sobriety marshalled our ranks as heretofore, and on the 29th the brigade quitted Benevente, but the cavalry remained in the town, leaving parties to watch the fords of the Esla. Soon after day-break, General Lefebre Desnouettes, seeing only a few cavalry-posts on the great plain, rather hastily concluded that there was nothing to support them, and crossing the river at a ford a little way above the bridge, with six hundred horsemen of the Imperial Guards, he advanced into the plain. The piquets at first retired fighting; but being joined by a part of the 3rd German Hussars, they charged the leading French squadron with some effect. General C. Stewart then took the command, and the ground was obstinately disputed. At this moment the plain was covered with stragglers, and baggage-mules, and followers of the army; the town was filled with tumult; the distant piquets and videttes were seen galloping in from the right and left; the French were pressing forward boldly, and every appearance indicated that the enemy's whole army was come up, and passing the river.

Lord Paget ordered the 10th Hussars to mount and form under the cover of some houses at the edge of the town: he desired to draw the enemy, whose real situation he saw at once, well into the plain before he attacked. In half an hour, every thing being ready, he gave the signal: the 10th Hussars galloped forward, the piquets that were already engaged, closed together, and the whole charged. In an instant the scene changed, the enemy were seen flying at full speed towards the river, and the British close at their heels. The French squadron, without breaking their ranks, plunged into the stream, and gained the opposite heights, where, like experienced soldiers, they wheeled instantly, and seemed inclined to come forward a second time; but a battery of six guns being opened upon them, after a few rounds, they retired.

During the pursuit in the plain, an officer was observed separating from the main body, and making towards another part of the river: being followed, and refusing to stop when overtaken, he was cut across the head, and brought in a prisoner. He proved to be General Lefebre. In this spirited action the French left fifty-five killed and wounded on the field, and seventy prisoners, besides the General, and other officers. The British loss was also severe.

Rencontres of this sort had their value, as they served to curb the audacity of the enemy and furnished a seasonable sample of what might be expected in the event of a general battle. Meantime the tide of superior force, against whose overpowering number it was physically impossible to present an effective check, came rolling on in waves of gathering might. Napoleon had arrived at Valderas, Ney at Villator, and Lapisse at Touro. The French troops were worn down with fatigue, yet the Emperor still urged them forward. He flattered himself, and wished to persuade others, that he should intercept the retreat of the English at Astorga; but the destruction of the bridge of Castro Gonzalo had been so complete, that twenty-four hours were required to repair it, and the fords were now impassable. After all, the Emperor, with whom it was never safe to trifle, was near the accomplishment of his design; for scarcely had the rear of the British army quitted Astorga, when advanced parties of French soldiery appeared in view.

CHAPTER 7

Retreat

Upon the 1st of January, 1809, the Emperor Napoleon took possession of Astorga. On that day seventy thousand French infantry, ten thousand cavalry, and two hundred pieces of artillery, after many days of incessant marching, were thus united. The assemblage of this mighty force, while it evinced the energy of the French Monarch, attested also the genius of the English General, who, with a handful of men, had found means to arrest the course of the conqueror, and to draw him, with the flower of his army, to this remote and unimportant part of the Peninsula, at the moment when Portugal, and the fairest provinces of Spain, were prostrate before him.

That Sir John Moore intercepted the blow which was then descending on Spain, no man of honesty can deny; for what troops were there in the south to have resisted even for an instant the progress of a man, who in ten days, and in the depth of winter, crossing the snowy ridge of the Carpentinos, had traversed two hundred miles of hostile country, and transported fifty thousand men from Madrid to Astorga in a shorter time than a Spanish diligence would have taken to travel the same distance?

This stupendous march was rendered fruitless by the quickness of the adversary; but Napoleon, though he had failed to destroy the English army, resolved nevertheless to drive it from the Peninsula; and being himself recalled to France by tidings that the Austrian storm was ready to burst, he fixed upon the Duke of Dalmatia to continue the pursuit, adding, for this purpose, three divisions of cavalry, and three of infantry, to his command. This formidable pursuing force was separated into three divisions, and entrusted to the command of Laborde, Heudelet, and Loison; so that after leaving a considerable corps in reserve in the Montagna de St. Andre, nearly sixty thousand men, and ninety-one guns, were put on the track of the English army.

About this period of the retreat an affair took place in the rear which excited the admiration of all who heard of it, and has seldom been exceeded for cool and determined valour under circumstances the most disadvantageous. So rapid were the advances of the British troops on their route to Corunna, that none but men of athletic mould and vigorous health could keep in column. As an unavoidable result, many of the weaker men, and some that had been overtaken by sickness, were at some distance behind. The number of stragglers thus compelled to fall out was nearly five hundred. They were placed under the direction of Sergeant William Newman, no other officer being present. In addition to the personal ailments of these poor fellows, they were little more than half clothed, and many of them barefooted, so that but for their muskets, which they knew how to handle, they exhibited an appearance altogether pitiable and defenceless.

Shortly after the army had quitted the village of Betanzos, an alarm was given that the French cavalry was approaching, when the men were instantly thrown into confusion by an eager but fruitless endeavour to overtake the British forces. In this exigence, Sergeant Newman pushed on a little way to a narrow part of the road. He there managed to hasten on the most feeble of the detachment, and detained about a hundred of the best men, whom he ordered to face about and contest the passage. This was promptly done, and with complete success. The little corps of invalids, consisting of soldiers from different regiments, withstood and repelled repeated attacks of the French horsemen.

The Sergeant then gave orders to retire, and when again pressed, reformed as before, and again repulsed the enemy. In this spirited manner they covered the retreat of their helpless comrades for four miles, when they were relieved from their perilous situation by the rear-guard of the British cavalry. It is pleasing to add, that the intrepid Sergeant who led this spirited movement, was promoted to an ensigncy in the 1st West India regiment; besides which, by way of putting him in gentlemanly trim, a gift was added of fifty pounds sterling.

Thus Sir John Moore was pressed in his retreat with fury that seemed to increase every moment. The separation of the light brigade already alluded to, a measure which he adopted by advice of the Quarter-Master General, weakened the army by three thousand men. Fifteen days only had elapsed since Sir John Moore had left Salamanca; and already the torrent of war, diverted from the south, was foaming among the rocks of Gallicia. Nineteen thousand British troops, if posted on strong ground, might have offered battle to very superior numbers; but where was the use of merely fighting an enemy who had three hundred thousand men in Spain? Sir John Moore felt the impolicy and rashness of such an attempt; his resolution therefore was, to fall down to the coast, and embark with as little loss and delay as might be. Vigo, Corunna, and Ferrol were the principal harbours, and their relative advantage could be determined only by the reports of the engineers, none of which had yet been received, so rapidly did the crisis of affairs come on.

It will be imagined by every person, civil or military, that the mind of a Commander, though of the firmest texture, in the situation of Sir John Moore, must have been severely exercised; and during this stage of the retreat the unavoidable difficulties of the army were inflamed by the unhappy intemperance of several who ought to have known and acted better.

On arriving at Bembibre, the immense wine-vaults established there exhibited such temptations, that hundreds of the men, unable to exert themselves, or even to stand, were unavoidably left behind. That refreshment was needed, no one can doubt; but it is more difficult to be temperate than abstemious; the first healthful draught led to many an inordinate one. Confusion worse confounded was the necessary result. There was an heterogeneous mass of marauders, drunkards, muleteers, women, and children: the weather was dreadful; and notwithstanding the utmost exertions of the superior officers, when the reserve marched next morning, the number of these unfortunate persons was not diminished.

Leaving a small guard to protect this bacchanalian crew, Sir John Moore proceeded to Calcabellos; and scarcely had the reserve marched out of the village, when some French cavalry appeared. In a moment the road was filled with the miserable stragglers, who came crowding after the troops, some with loud shrieks of distress, others with brutal exclamations. Many, overcome with fear, threw away their arms. Many more who preserved theirs, were so stupidly intoxicated that they were unable to fire; and kept reeling to and fro, insensible both to their danger and disgrace.

The enemy's horsemen, perceiving this confusion, bore down at a gallop, broke through the disorderly mob, cutting to the right and left as they passed, and riding so close to the columns, that the infantry were forced to halt in order to check their forwardness. Nothing, in the nature of things, can be more mischievous, though it endure only for a day, or even half that time, than such a violation of discipline as that recorded. It not only tends to produce discouragement in the ranks of well-ordered troops, whose resolution, founded on mutual support, is by such means sadly assailed, but so far

as it is observed, and it can seldom be concealed, it gives pro-
portionate confidence to the enemy, of which, on this very
occasion, there was almost instantaneous proof.

On the 3rd of January, 1809, just after mid-day, the French
General, Colbert, approached with six or eight squadrons;
but observing the ground behind Calcabellos strongly occupied, he demanded reinforcements. Marshal Soult, believing the English did not mean to make a stand, sent orders
to Colbert to charge without delay. The latter, stung by the
message, which he thought conveyed an imputation on his
courage, obeyed with precipitate fury. The Riflemen had
withdrawn when the French first came in sight, and were
just passing the bridge when a crowd of staff officers, the
cavalry, and the enemy, came in upon them in one mass. In
the confusion, thirty or forty men were taken; and Colbert,
crossing the river, charged on the spur up the road. The remainder of the Riflemen threw themselves into the vineyards, and permitting the enemy to approach within a few
yards, suddenly opened such a deadly fire, that the greater
number of the French horsemen were killed on the spot,
and among the rest Colbert himself. His fine martial figure,
his voice, his gestures, and, above all, his daring valour, had
excited the admiration of the British, and a general feeling
of sorrow prevailed when he fell, The French Voltigeurs then
crossed the river, and a smart skirmish was maintained, in
which two or three hundred men on both sides were killed
or wounded. Night put an end to the combat.

The reserve at length reached Nogales, having by a forced
march of thirty-six miles gained twelve hours' start of the
enemy; but at this period of retreat the road was crowded
with stragglers and baggage; the peasantry, although armed,
did not molest the French; but fearing both sides alike, drove
their cattle and carried away their effects into the mountains on each side of the line of march. Under the most
favourable circumstances, the drooping portion of a retreat-

ing force indicates sensible distress; and on the road near Nogales the followers of the army were dying fast from cold and hunger. The soldiers, barefooted, harassed, and weakened by their excesses at Bembibre and Villa Franca, were dropping to the rear by hundreds. Broken carts, dead animals, and the piteous appearance of women with children, struggling or falling in the snow, completed the picture of war and its desolating results.

On the evening of the 4th the French recovered their lost ground, and passed Nogales, galling the rear-guard with a continual skirmish. Here it was that dollars to the amount of twenty-five thousand pounds were abandoned. This small sum was kept near headquarters, to answer sudden emergencies; and the bullocks that drew it being tired, the General, who could not save the money without risking an ill-timed action, had it rolled down the side of a mountain. Part of it was gathered by the enemy, and part by the Gallician peasantry.

After exchanging several shots with the enemy, wherever appearances called for resistance, the army retired to Lugo, in front of which the entire force was assembled; and on the 7th of January Sir John Moore announced his intention to offer battle. Scarcely was the order issued, when the line of battle, hitherto so peeled and spread abroad, was filled with vigorous men, full of confidence and courage. At day-break on the 8th the two armies were still embattled. On the French side seventeen thousand infantry, four thousand cavalry, and fifty pieces of artillery were in line; but Soult deferred the attack till the 9th. On the English side sixteen thousand infantry, eighteen hundred cavalry, and forty pieces of artillery, awaited the assault. No advance was, however, made; darkness fell without a shot being fired; and with it the English General's hope of engaging his enemy on equal terms.

This was a season of singular and almost unexampled peril. The French were posted on the declivity of a precipitous range of mountains with a numerous body of cavalry to protect their infantry, wherever necessary. Besides this, twenty thousand fresh troops were at the distance of two short marches in the rear. Then it should be considered that the British army was not in a condition to fight more than one battle. It was unprovided with draught cattle, had no means of transporting reserve ammunition, no magazines, no hospitals, no second line, no provisions.

In the opinion of competent judges a defeat would have been irretrievably ruinous, and a victory of no real use. Some have suggested that Sir John Moore might have remained longer in expectation of a battle. That was not only inexpedient, but impossible. The state of the magazine; decided the matter; for there was not bread for another day's consumption in the stores at Lugo. It is true the soldiers ware at the moment in fighting mood; but want of necessary food would have deprived them of physical energy; so that to expose an army of gallant but starving men to the uncertain issue of an obstinate and probably prolonged engagement, would not only have been absurd in policy, but have amounted to a wanton and unmeaning waste of human life. An effort, therefore, to gain a march as quietly as possible, and get on board without molestation, or at least so to establish the army as to cover the embarkation, was the most, if not the only, reasonable proposition to which prudence ought to listen.

The General adopted this third plan and prepared to decamp in the night. He ordered the fires to be kept bright, and exhorted the troops to make a great effort, which he trusted would be the last required of them. The face of the country immediately in the rear of the position was intersected by stone walls, and a number of intricate lanes. Precautions were taken to mark the right track by placing bundles of straw at certain distances, and officers were appointed to guide the columns. At ten o'clock the troops silently quitted their ground, and retired in excellent order; but at this critical juncture a terrible storm of wind and rain arose, so that the marks were destroyed, and the guides lost the true direction. Only one of the divisions gained the main road; the other two were bewildered; and when day-light broke, the rear columns were still near Lugo.

The fatigue and depression of mind occasioned by this misfortune, and the want of shoes especially, contributed to break the order of the march, and the stragglers were becoming numerous, when, unhappily, one of the Generals commanding a leading division, thinking to relieve the men during a nightly halt, desired them to take refuge from the weather in some houses a little way off the road.

Complete disorder followed this untimely indulgence: from that moment it became impossible to make the soldiers of the division keep their ranks; and in this disastrous condition the main body of the army, which had bivouacked for six hours in the rain, arrived at Betanzos on the evening of the 9th.

During the two following days Sir John Moore was indefatigable in restoring the needful order and discipline. He assembled the army in one solid mass. The loss of men in the march from Lugo to Betanzos had been greater than in all the former part of the retreat; so that the infantry then in column did not much exceed fourteen thousand men.

Chapter 8

Corunna

As the troops approached Corunna, many an anxious look was directed towards the harbour. *Nothing was to be discovered but the wide waste of water.* The painful truth became evident, that contrary winds had detained at Vigo the fleet on board of whose ships the forces sought to embark; so that after one of the severest and most prolonged tests to which human endurance could be submitted, and the consuming exertions, pushed on through storm and tempest, of many wearisome days, the whole was rendered nugatory by an event over which human foresight or power had no control; and the point to which they had fought their way, instead of presenting the means of effectual retreat, became a *cul de sac,* or place leading nowhere.

The men were immediately put into quarters, and their leader awaited the progress of events. Three divisions occupied the town and suburbs: the reserve was posted with its left at the village of El Burgo, and its right on the road of St. Jago de Compostella. For twelve days these hardy soldiers had covered the retreat, during which time they had traversed eighty miles of road in two marches, passed several nights under arms in the snow of the mountains, were seven times engaged with the enemy; and they now assembled at the outposts, having fewer men missing from the ranks than any other division of the army.

The bridge of El Burgo was immediately destroyed, and an engineer was sent to blow up that of Combria, situated a few miles up the Mero river. This officer was mortified at the former failures, and so anxious to perform his duty in an effectual manner, that lie remained too near the mine, and was killed by the explosion. This was followed by the destruction of an immense quantity of combustible material. Three miles from the town four thousand barrels of powder were piled in a magazine built on a hill; a smaller quantity collected in another storehouse was at some distance from the first: to prevent these magazines from falling into the hands of the enemy, they were both fired on the 13th. The inferior one blew up with a terrible noise, and shook the houses in the town; but when the train reached the great store, there ensued a crash like the bursting forth of a volcano; the earth trembled for miles; the rocks were torn from their bases, and the agitated waters rolled the vessels as in a storm. A vast column of smoke and dust, shooting out fiery sparks from its sides, arose perpendicularly and slowly to a great height, and then a shower of stones and fragments of all kinds bursting out of it with a roaring sound, killed several persons who remained too near the spot. A stillness, interrupted only by the lashing of the waves on the shore, succeeded, and the business of the war went on.

The plot now rapidly thickened. Hemmed in by the gathering forces of the numerous French corps, whose advance had been hastened by prodigious sacrifices, both of men and means, the handful of British troops, thinned by recent losses, and worn down by the length of a harassed and contested march, were now cooped within the surface of a few square miles. Negotiation with the enemy, having for its object the permissive embarkation of the army, had been intimated to the Commander by some of the officers as a prudent step, under the continued and increasing difficulties of the army, but was properly rejected, with that high spirit and clear judgement which was safely founded on an intimate knowledge of the army he commanded, and the resistance it could offer, even in its dangerous and unfavourable position.

The enemy having collected in force on the Mero, it became necessary to choose a position of battle. A chain of rocky elevations, commencing on the sea-coast, and ending on the Mero, just behind the village of El Burgo, offered an advantageous line of defence; but this ridge was too extensive for the British army, and, if not wholly occupied, the French might have turned it by the right, and moved along a succession of eminences to the gates of Corunna. There was no alternative but to take post on an inferior range, enclosed, as it were, within the other, and completely commanded by it within cannon shot. The French army had been so exhausted by toil, that it was not completely assembled on the Mero before the 12th.

The same evening the expected transports from Vigo hove in sight, and soon after entered the harbour of Corunna; and the dismounted cavalry, the sick, all the best of the horses, and fifty-two pieces of artillery, were embarked during the night: eight British and four Spanish guns were, however, retained on shore, ready for action.

Towards evening on the 15th, the English piquets opposite the right of the French got engaged, and being galled by the fire of two guns, Colonel McKenzie, of the 5th, at the head of some companies, endeavoured to seize the battery, when a line of infantry, hitherto concealed by some stone walls, arose, and poured in such a fire of musketry, that the Colonel was killed, and his men forced back with loss.

The morning of the 16th at length arose. All the encumbrances of the army had been shipped on the preceding night, and every measure that prudence could suggest was adopted for the safe and expeditious embarkation of the men, whenever the darkness would permit them to move without being perceived; but about two o'clock in the afternoon every one saw that these preparations, though skilfully arranged, would not then be required.

A general movement along the French line gave notice of immediate action, and nothing remained on our side but to give them a proper reception. The British infantry, fourteen thousand five hundred strong, occupied the inferior range of hills already named. The French force could not be less than twenty thousand men; and the Duke of Dalmatia, having made his disposition, lost little time in idle evolutions. His lighter guns being distributed along the front of his line, a heavy fire was opened from the battery on his left, when three solid masses of infantry led to the assault.

A cloud of skirmishers led the way, and the British piquets being driven back in disorder, the village of Elvina was carried by the first column, which afterwards dividing, one half pushed on against Baird's front, the other turned his right by the valley. The second column made for the centre. The third engaged the left by the village of Palavia Abaxo. The weight of the French guns over matched the English six-pounders, and their shot swept the position to the centre. The ground about the village of Elvina was intersected by stone walls and hollow roads: a severe scrambling fight ensued, but in half an hour the French were borne back with great loss. The 50th regiment entered the village with them, and after a second struggle, drove them to some distance beyond it.

Meanwhile the General, bringing up a battalion of the brigade of Guards to fill the space in the line left vacant by those two regiments, the 42nd mistook his intentions, and at that moment the enemy, being reinforced, renewed the fight beyond the village; the officer commanding the 50th was wounded and taken prisoner, and Elvina became the scene of another struggle. This being observed by the Commander-in-Chief, he addressed a few animating words to the 42nd, and caused it to return to the attack. General Paget,

With the reserve, now descended into the valley, and the line of skirmishers, being thus supported, vigorously checked the advance of the enemy's troops in that quarter, while the 4th regiment galled their flank. A furious action now ensued along the entire line, in the valley, and on the hills.

Sir John Moore, while earnestly watching the result of the battle about the village of Elvina, was struck on the left breast by a cannon shot. The shock threw him from his horse with violence. He rose again in a sitting posture. His eye was still fixed on the regiments engaged in his front; and in a few moments, when he was satisfied that the troops were gaining ground, his countenance brightened, and he suffered himself to be taken to the rear. The dreadful nature of the injury he had received was then noticed; the shoulder was shattered in pieces, and the muscles of the breast torn into long strips, which were interlaced by their recoil from the strain and dragging of the shot. As the soldiers placed him in a blanket his sword got entangled, and the hilt entered the wound. Captain Hardinge, a staff officer, who was near, attempted to take it off; but the dying man stopped him, saying, "It is as well as it is. I had rather it should go out of the field with me." In that manner Sir John was borne from the fight.

During this time the army was rapidly gaining ground. The reserve, overthrowing every thing in the valley, and obliging Houssaye's dragoons, who had dismounted, to re-tire, turned the enemy's left, and even approached the emi-nence upon which the great battery was erected. On the left, Colonel Nicholls, at the head of some companies of the 14th, carried Palavia Abaxo, and in the centre the obstinate dispute for Elvina terminated in favour of the British; so that when the night set in, their line was considerably beyond the position of the morning, and the French were falling back in confusion. On the other hand, to continue the action in the dark was a dangerous experiment; for the French were still the most numerous, and their ground was strong.

The disorder they were in, offered so favourable an opportunity to get on board the ships, that Sir John Hope, upon whom the command of the army had devolved, satisfied with having repulsed the attack, judged it more prudent to pursue the original plan of embarking during the night: that operation was effected without delay the arrangements being complete, no confusion or difficulty occurred. The piquets kindling a number of fires covered the retreat of the columns, and were themselves withdrawn at day-break, and embarked under the protection of General Hill's brigade, which was posted near the ramparts of the town.

When the morning dawned, the French, observing that the British had abandoned their position, pushed forward some battalions to the height of St. Lucie, and succeeded in establishing a battery, which, playing upon the shipping in the harbour; caused a great deal of disorder among the transports. Several masters cut their cables, and four vessels went on shore; but the troops being immediately removed by the men-of-war's boats, the stranded vessels were burnt, and the whole fleet at last got away. Thus ended the retreat to Corunna. From the spot where he fell, the General who commanded it was carried to the town by a party of soldiers; the blood flowed fast, and the torture of the wound increased, but such was the firmness of his mind that those about him expressed a hope that his hurt was not mortal. Hearing this, he looked steadfastly at the injury for a moment, and then said, "No, I feel that to be impossible."

Several times he caused his attendants to stop and turn him round, that he might behold the field of battle; and when the firing indicated the advance of the British, he expressed his satisfaction, and permitted the bearers to proceed. Being brought to his lodgings, the surgeons examined the wound; but there was no hope: the pain increased, and he spake with great difficulty. His countenance continued firm, and his thoughts clear; only once, when he spake of his mother, he became agitated. The fight was scarcely ended, when his corpse, wrapped in a military cloak, was interred by the officers of his staff in the citadel of Corunna. The guns of the enemy paid his funeral honours; and Soult, with a noble feeling of respect for his valour, raised a monument to his memory.

Through the whole of this eventful retreat, I was mercifully preserved from grievous injury. The privations of the army were shared by all; and to these I was no stranger. Many miles of road through which our route lay were nearly deserted by the inhabitants, who, unknowing whom to trust, were afraid both of friend and foe: hence arose great scarcity of provisions. It often happened that long before we had appeared, tidings of our approach had induced the entire population of the district to disappear, and with it all vestiges of food. Wine might occasionally be obtained, and sometimes in profusion; but I had observed that when our men had indulged in strong liquor, with little or no solid food, the effect was injurious, so that on the following day, when the excitement had subsided, they were unable to keep our pace: diminished strength thus compelled them to drop off, and not a few were actually picked up by the French who hung on our rear. Another serious difficulty arose from the circumstance that our retreat was conducted in winter: the roads for an immense distance had been torn into deep ruts by the wheels of the baggage-wagons and cannon, and tendered rough by the trampling of cavalry horses; severe frost then set in, when the rough and rugged surface was suddenly hardened into ice.

Meantime my shoes were worn out, and as they would no longer hold together, I was compelled to march barefooted: this was severe, and the sensation produced was singularly painful. In the frozen condition of the ground every step seemed to place my feet on flint: scarcely able to move, and yet forbidden to stay, the Sergeant of my company, a worthy fellow, proposed to lend me a pair of shoes, but his kindness was unavailing; on attempting to put them on, they would not fit my feet. How it was that I was sustained under these difficulties, I knew not then; but now I know: the Almighty was my support, though I was heedless of his help. I feel at this moment some satisfaction, which I hope may be pardoned, that though heavily pressed with the sufferings of those days, I never fell out of the line of march, or impeded the public service by imbecility of purpose, or disposition to flinch from duty. Previous to embarkation I was provided with the article needed; and, praised be the Lord, I have never wanted a pair of shoes from that day to this. On getting into the boat which conveyed me on board the ship, determined to forget my former vexations, I threw my old shoes into the sea, and there, like my past troubles, they were soon out of sight and forgotten.

CHAPTER 9

Experiences on the March

During a violent snow-storm, which overtook us on our march upon Corunna, several of my comrades, and myself among the rest, wearied with fatigue, took refuge one evening in a small out-house or hovel, as it afforded temporary shelter from the descending storm. There we resolved to pass the night; and having gathered a few sticks, we placed them in the middle of the shed, and kindled a fire for mutual benefit. In the course of the night we were surprised by hearing a rap at the door, accompanied by the weak tone of some one craving admission. Half a dozen voices instantly exclaimed, "Come in:" when, lo! a woman, recognised as the wife of a soldier, but hardly able to stand, crept into the shed, and asked protection from the hurricane that was loudly howling along the sierra: had Satan himself begged an entrance at such a moment, we should scarcely have been able to repress our pity.

The poor wandering woman was received with rough but honest sympathy, and was invited to approach the fire. When able to speak she asked for a certain company, to which her husband belonged: we told her it was considerably in advance, and at present out of her reach. Modesty prevented the poor creature from further explanation; when; to the surprise of the men present, the weak cry of a child was heard. The fact was, the mother had in the course of the preceding day given birth to an infant while on the snowy ridge of a desolate mountainous tract, and without the company of a single human being: and yet, so far all was well:— there is One who tempers the wind to the shorn lamb. The life both of the mother and her offspring was whole; and though in a condition so extraordinary, they were likely to survive.

English soldiers know how to feel, nor are they quite destitute of discretion; they may be rather rough in manner, nor can they at all times invent the phraseology of oily compliment; but they have no part of the bear about them except the skin, unless provoked, and then the consequences must be abided: when virtue is in distress, none can show sympathy with greater delicacy, or exercise benevolence with more perfect freedom. At the appearance and sad tale of this suffering daughter of affliction, every heart in the place was touched: wretched as was our own condition, each man contrived to spare something. They even parted with some article of their own linen, much as they needed it, for the purpose of contributing to the warmth and comfort of the sufferer: kindness of speech was added, and it did wonders.

While on our march the following day the woman, again on her feet, was observed by one of our officers: he was told the story of her distress, and, with kindness which none but a great and gallant heart possesses, he alighted from his horse and tramped with us in favour of the poor woman and child. The animal, like his master, joined in the scheme, and carried his novel load most comfortably. I rejoice to add, that both root and branch were preserved, and eventually transplanted in the soil at home.

Let me be permitted here to relate the particulars of another circumstance, the truth of which is attested by evidence which none need doubt. Not long before our arrival at Corunna, and in the severest part of the retreat, Surgeon Griffith, of the Dragoons, while riding at a rapid pace, observed a woman with a child, reclining on the snow: the weather was tempestuous, and the advanced posts of the enemy not far in the rear. Humanity, however, compelled him to notice the unfortunate female: he immediately reined in his horse and dismounted, when he discovered with regret, that the woman now stretched upon the ground had just breathed her last. She had dropped, no doubt, and perished like many others from mere exhaustion; while the infant, all unconscious of the calamity, had nestled his head close to the cold bosom of his hapless mother, and was endeavouring to suck as heretofore.

The melancholy spectacle had now fully aroused the compassion of the horseman, and as relief came too late for the parent, he determined if possible to save the child. He accordingly lifted him up, and after placing him comfortably on the saddle, again mounted and rode on.

The apprehended danger was soon realized: having lost time by this merciful act, he was overtaken by the enemy's cavalry, by whom he and the child were captured and ordered to the rear. This good Samaritan was, however, faithful to his charge, and he and the infant, though prisoners, were inseparable companions. After being detained so time in France, and having visited Paris, Griffith obtained his liberty on parole, and proceeded to England.

The tender little child had by this time grown into a healthy boy, and was placed by the interest of his benefactor in the Military Asylum at Chelsea. Even here his kind attentions were continued; he generally paid the lad a Sabbath-day visit, and never failed to bring him a present either for his instruction or amusement, not forgetting to line his pocket with a little of the needful for passing exigencies.

About three years after the occurrence just related, a soldier who had lost his wife and child in Spain, came to the Asylum at Chelsea to inquire concerning the welfare of a son of his named Hector, who had been previously placed in the establishment. The veteran had not long been engaged in conversation with Hector when the attention of the former was excited by the appearance of a younger lad, in whose countenance there were lines on which his sight seemed to be unavoidably riveted. On consideration, the features were more familiar than ever: the thought then arose, "Perhaps this may be my long-lost child who I deemed had perished in the snow." The father recollected that on a particular place just above one of the knees, his child had a scar; and on raising the boy's trousers, there it was! The two brothers, though unknown, had been playfellows, and were mutually attached. The delights of this singular recognition may be better conceived than described.

CHAPTER 10
Talavera

On the 18th of January, 1809, we left the shores of Spain, and made the voyage home on board the *Hindostan*, of sixty-four guns, which had been partially cut down and prepared as a transport. We encountered several heavy gales during the passage, but were mercifully preserved from a watery grave. It was on a Sabbath evening that the lighthouse near Plymouth became visible from deck: it is built on a ledge of rock, about eighteen miles from the harbour, and gave us cheering proof that we were nearing the land we loved. After remaining at anchor for a short time, it was judged advisable to proceed up the Channel; we accordingly weighed, and stood for Portsmouth, at which place the shattered remains of our regiment were safely landed. Aware of the deplorable figure we made, the debarkation was cleverly effected under cover of the night.

The pride which urged this method was, I trust, excusable: such a legion of ragged warriors I should think never before approached this or any other land; we were therefore glad to escape observation, and march quickly into barracks. Our old clothes, by far too bad for amendment, were speedily burned, together with a countless company of Spanish insects thereunto appertaining, and which, to our oft-repeated sorrow, we were never able fully to eject. A few weeks' residence on shore restored us to society and our friends; and in a period of time marvellously short we held ourselves ready for service either at home or abroad.

Time rolled rapidly away, and though our stay in England was extended to the space of several months, such was the buoyancy of our spirits, and the general hilarity, that it had passed like a summer's day. The business of recruiting our ranks had gone on so rapidly that by the end of May we mustered a thousand rank and file; nor were our arms in the least danger of contracting rust: firing at a target was an every day exercise; field-days were frequently appointed, and the note of warlike preparation was familiar and agreeable.

I am sorry to say that my boasting can not extend to the morals of my friends. Cards and dice, with other games of chance, connected with the intemperance and dissipation of which they are the usual forerunners, consumed the time of most of those by whom I was surrounded. From these excesses I was preserved; and if asked by what means, I can only reply, that I felt an aversion to such practices, grounded, I firmly believe, upon the advices once received from my honoured mother, which as a warning and monitory voice pursued and protected me through life, and by which, though far away, she seemed to speak the words of wisdom. The regularity of my conduct, as a private soldier, attracted the notice of the officers, and I had the satisfaction of hearing that there was some probability of an elevation from the place I held in the ranks to that of a Corporal in the British army,—a distinction to which my wishes were earnestly directed.

Having remained some time at Colchester, orders were received towards the close of May to march to the coast. We accordingly proceeded to Harwich, and immediately embarked. With the exception of the inconveniences arising from crowded berths, and provisions of very defective quality, nothing occurred to ruffle the good humour that prevailed between decks during the passage.

In little more than thirty days from the time of leaving home we were released from our confinement on shipboard. It was a pleasing sound when the man on look-out exclaimed, "Land a-head." In the course of a few hours we passed the castle of St. Julian, and soon after rode at anchor in the Tagus, from whence we were conveyed in boats to Villa Franca and Santarem. The latter is a fine large town, commanding a noble view of the adjacent country. The weather was extremely hot, and water scarce. Wine was cheap, three pints of which could be obtained for about fourpence.

Anxious to form a junction with the forces under Sir Arthur Wellesley, who, it was rightly conjectured, might be engaged with the enemy, our march was urged by every possible means. We suffered in consequence very severely. Over head the scorching rays of an almost vertical sun appeared to wither the face of nature, while the hot sand on which we trod blistered and inflamed our feet, By uncommon exertion we reached Abrantes, where we found a small encampment, formerly occupied, but hastily abandoned, by the French.

Ready to drop as most of us were, the halt, though short, was grateful, and of great value. After a brief stay, our march was renewed with greater speed than before; and as the nights were comparatively cool, we advanced without intermission. Proofs that hard fighting had commenced now crowded on us on every side. We met several dastardly renegade Spaniards, who asserted that the British forces were defeated, and all was lost. Scattered groups of men were also occasionally seen silently retiring. The muttering of distant artillery had been heard for some time; but these indications of actual contest, so far from dispiriting our party, called forth redoubled exertions to press forward.

Our pace increased to a kind of impetuous movement, which, by tacit agreement, was to be neither retarded nor turned aside. The result was, that though three thousand strong, with the exception of seventeen stragglers left behind, one of whom was well thrashed with some olive-twigs for leaving the ranks, we had, in twenty-six hours crossed the field of battle in a close and compact body, and passed over sixty-two English miles, in the hottest season of the year, each man carrying from fifty to sixty pounds weight upon his shoulders. It is not for me to boast; but if this was not stepping out with spirit, I should like to know what is.

Our arrival was hailed as an auspicious omen; for though too late to take any part in the battle of Talavera, which had just been fought, our presence served to exhilarate the army, which, though victorious, required support. The fight had been well sustained on both sides. From nine o'clock in the morning until mid-day the field of battle offered no appearance of hostility; the weather was intensely hot, and the troops on both sides descended and mingled, without fear or suspicion, to quench their thirst at the little brook which divided the positions; but at one o'clock in the afternoon the French soldiers were seen to gather round their eagles, and the rolling of drums was heard along the whole line.

Half an hour later the Guards of King Joseph, the reserve, and the 4th corps, were descried near the centre of the enemy's position, marching to join the 1st corps; and at two o'clock the table-land, and the height on the French right, even to the valley, were covered with the dark and lowering masses. The Duke of Belluno, whose arrangements were now completed, gave the signal for battle; and eighty pieces of artillery immediately sent out a tempest of bullets before the light troops, who, coming on swiftly, and with the violence of a hailstorm, were closely followed by the broad black columns, in all the majesty of war.

Sir Arthur Wellesley, from the summit of the hill, had a clear view of the entire scene of action. He saw the 4th corps rush forward with the usual celerity of French soldiers, and, clearing the entrenched ground in their front, fall upon Campbell's division with prodigious fury; but that General, assisted by Mackenzie's brigade, and by two Spanish battalions, withstood their utmost efforts. The English regiments putting the French skirmishers aside, met the advancing columns with loud shouts, and, breaking in on their front, and lapping their flanks with fire, and giving no respite, pushed them back with terrible carnage. Ten guns were taken; but, as General Campbell prudently forbore pursuit, the French rallied on their supports, and made a show of attacking again, but did not attempt it.

The British artillery and musketry were directed with vehement accuracy against their masses, and a Spanish regiment of cavalry charging on their flank at the same time, the whole retired in disorder, and the victory was secured in that quarter. The next grand attack was directed to the English centre, which was thrown into great confusion, and for some time completely broken.

The late of the day for some moments seemed to incline in favour of the French, when suddenly Colonel Donellan, with the 48th regiment, was seen advancing through the midst of the disordered masses. At first it appeared as if this regiment must be carried away by the retiring crowds; but, wheeling back by companies, it let them pass through the intervals, and then, resuming its firm and beautiful line, marched against the right of the pursuing columns, plied them with such a destructive musketry, and closed upon them with a pace so regular and steady, that the forward movement of the French was checked. The Guards and the Germans immediately rallied; a brigade of light cavalry came up from the second line at a trot; the artillery battered the enemy's flanks without intermission, and the French, beginning to waver, soon lost their advantage, and the battle was restored.

The annals of warfare often tell us that in all actions there is one critical and decisive moment which will give the victory to the General who knows how to discover and secure it. When the Guards first made their rash charge, Sir Arthur

Wellesley, foreseeing the issue of it, had ordered the 48th down from the hill, although a rough battle was going on there, and at the same time he ordered Cotton's light cavalry to advance. These dispositions gained the day. The French relaxed their efforts by degrees; the fire of the English grew hotter; and their loud and confident shouts, sure augury of success, were heard along the whole line.

The French army soon after retired to the position from whence it had descended to the attack. This retrograde movement was covered by skirmishers, and increasing fire of artillery ; and the British, reduced to less than fourteen thousand men, and exhausted by toil and want of food, were unable to pursue. The battle was scarcely over when the dry grass and shrubs taking fire, a volume of flame passed with inconceivable rapidity across a part of the field, scorching in its course both the dead and wounded.

The loss of the British in the course of this severe action and previous skirmishing was upwards of six thousand men killed and wounded. That of the French, as afterwards appeared in a manuscript of Marshal Jourdan, was rather more than seven thousand three hundred.

The following morning presented a choice of disagreeables. Having taken a position along the battle field somewhat in advance of the British line, we were surrounded with the dying and the dead. The number of the latter was hourly increasing. Combatants who had mingled in the fray, belonging to either army, lay intermingled in frightful heaps. Many of the bodies, though exposed only for so short a time to the sun's rays, were offensively putrid and discoloured, so that interment without ceremony or distinction became necessary for the safety of the living.

Meantime provisions were scanty, the water we had to drink was stagnant, the heat of the weather increased, and the enemy was hastily concentrating in great force in the vicinity.

The 30th of July was passed by Sir Arthur in establishing hospitals at Talavera, and in fruitless endeavours to procure food, and the help required to keep the wounded men from perishing. On this occasion the Spanish behaved infamously. Not an inhabitant, although possessing ample means, would render the slightest aid, nor even assist to bury the dead. The corn secreted in Talavera alone was sufficient to support the army for a month; but the troops were starving, although the inhabitants, who had fled across the Tagus with their portable effects at the beginning of the battle, had returned. This conduct left an indelible impression on the minds of the English soldiers. From that period their contempt and dislike of the Spaniards were never effaced.

The principal motive in war with these people was personal rancour: hence those troops who had behaved so ill in action, and the inhabitants, who alike withheld their sympathy and their aid from the English soldiers, to whose bravery they owed the preservation of their town, were busily engaged after the battle in beating out the brains of the wounded French, as they lay upon the field; and they were only checked by the English soldiers, who, in some instances, fired upon the perpetrators of this horrible iniquity.

CHAPTER 11

Hard Campaigning

Hitherto the allied Generals had paid little attention to the Duke of Dalmatia's movements; but on the 30th of July information was received that he had entered Placentia at the head of an imposing force. The danger of the British on account of their numerical inferiority was extreme; in fact, the fate of the Peninsula was suspended on a thread, which the events of .a few hours might dissever; and yet it was so ordered that no irreparable disaster ensued.

The Generals on each side at length became acquainted with each other's strength; and this, it will be believed, was a moment of extreme peril for the British. Their progress was barred in front, the Tagus was on their left, impassable mountains on their right, and it was certain that the retreat of the Spanish would bring down the King and Victor upon their rear. In this trying moment Sir Arthur Wellesley abated nothing ill his usual calmness and fortitude. He knew not the full extent of the danger; but assuming the enemy in his front to be thirty thousand men, and Victor to have twenty-five thousand others in his rear, he judged that to continue the offensive would be rash, because he must fight and defeat those two Marshals separately within three days, which, with starving and tired troops, inferior in number, was scarcely to be accomplished.

The movements of Sir Arthur were executed with precision and success. About noon, the road being clear, the columns marched to the bridge, and at two o'clock the whole army was in position on the other side; the present danger was therefore averted, and the combinations of the enemy baffled.

Our sufferings during these rapid transitions were almost intolerable. During the passage several herds of swine were met with, feeding in the woods, when the soldiers ran in among the animals, shooting, stabbing, and, like men possessed, cutting off the flesh while the beasts were yet alive. Well has it been said that hunger will break through stone walls. I had carried a sheaf of wheat for many miles on my knapsack, rubbing the ears when opportunity offered between my hands, and eating the extracted grain with rapture. At night, by way of a feast, I used to thrash a little more, by bruising the grain, having first laid my great-coat on the ground for the purpose. On one occasion a comrade, by great exertion, procured a small quantity of bullock's blood. We agreed to boil it for dinner, and halve it between us. We did so; and, though unaided even by a bit of salt, I thought it delicious.

These privations occurred in our passage through an elevated and open tract of country, where shelter from the sultry heat could hardly be procured. One of these spots we called Mount Misery. Many a time we have breakfasted upon the acorns or oak-nuts beaten down by the Spanish swineherds for the use of the hogs. A goat's offal sold at this time for four dollars, or about double the usual price of the whole animal; and men and officers strove to outbid each other in the purchase of this wretched pittance. In one word, famine raged through the camp; and it was notorious that the Spanish cavalry intercepted the provisions and forage destined for the English army, and fired upon the foragers, as if they had been enemies.

From Arzobispo the army moved towards Deleytoza; and

our brigade, with six pieces of artillery, was directed to gain the bridge of Almarez by a forced march, lest the enemy, discovering the ford below that place, should cross the river, and seize the Puerto de Mirabete. The roads were rugged, and the guns could be drawn only by the force of men. The movement was, however, effected.

The Spaniards under Albuquerque were not equally successful. The infantry were sleeping or loitering about without care or thought, when Mortier, who was charged with the direction of the attack, taking advantage of their want of vigilance, commenced the passage of the river.

The French cavalry, about six thousand in number, were secretly assembled near the ford, and about two o'clock in the day General Caulincourt's brigade suddenly entered the stream. The Spanish, running to their arms, manned the batteries, and opened upon the leading squadrons; but Mortier, with a powerful concentric fire of artillery, overwhelmed the Spanish gunners, and dispersed the infantry who attempted to form. On the 20th of August the main body of the British army quitted Jaraicejo, and marched by Truxillo upon Merida. Our brigade, under General Crauford, being relieved at Almarez by the Spaniards, took the road of Caceres to Valencia de Alcantara; but the pass of Mirabete discovered how much we had suffered.

Our brigade, which only a few weeks before, had traversed sixty miles in a single march, were now with difficulty, and after many halts, only able to reach the summit of the Mirabete, although only four miles from the camp; and the side of that mountain was covered with baggage, and the carcases of many hundred animals that died in the ascent. In this eventful campaign of two months, the loss of the army was considerable. Above three thousand five hundred men had been killed, or had died of sickness, or had fallen into the hands of the enemy. Fifteen hundred horses had perished for want of food; and, to fill the bitter cup, the pestilent fever of the Guadiana, assailing those who by fatigue and bad nourishment were predisposed to disease, made frightful ravages. Dysentery, that scourge of armies, also raged, and in a short time above five thousand men died in the hospitals.

CHAPTER 12

The Progress of the War

Passing by the details of successive conflicts sustained with unequal success by the Spanish forces in opposing their invaders. It may be sufficient generally to state, that their inability to maintain the defensive positions assumed, without English cooperation, was evident. An attempt was at length made by the French forces, under Marshal Victor, to gain possession of Cadiz, situate in the Isle of Leon, in Andalusia, the finest port in Spain, with a mercantile and wealthy population of an hundred and fifty thousand inhabitants. For this purpose preparations of extraordinary magnitude were made. The assaulting army was spread quite round the margin of the harbour. Works of contravallation were constructed not less than twenty-five miles in extent, and strong batteries frowned upon the city wherever they could be erected with advantage to the besiegers. The lines of blockade were connected by a covered way concealed by thick woods, and when finished mounted three hundred guns.

On the other hand, the Spanish troops under Albuquerque, composing the garrison, were in a miserable condition. The whole had been long without pay, and the greater part without arms or accoutrements. Men were placed in command destitute of energy or local influence, and private traffic was unblushingly pursued with the public stores. Albuquerque was afterwards sent Ambassador to England, where he died soon after of a frenzy, brought on, it is said, by grief and passion at the unworthy treatment he received.

In this deplorable state of affairs, British troops again appeared, and the surrender of the city by that means was averted. On the 11th of February, 1810, General Stewart arrived in Cadiz with three thousand men, who were received with enthusiastic joy. On the 17th of the same month, thirteen hundred Portuguese arrived, and Spanish troops in small bodies came in daily. Two ships of war, the *Euthalion* and *Undaunted*, arrived from Mexico, with six millions of dollars: and other British troops having appeared, the whole force assembled behind the Santa Petri was not fewer than eighteen thousand effective men.

The worst symptom was, that among the Spaniards there was little enthusiasm, and not a man among the citizens had been enrolled or armed, or had volunteered either to labour or fight. General Stewart's first measure was to recover Matagorda, a most important point, about four thousand yards from the city, which the Spaniards had foolishly dismantled and abandoned.

In the night of the 22nd a detachment, consisting of fifty marines and seamen, twenty-five artillery-men, and sixty-seven of the 94th regiment, the whole under the command of Captain McLean, pushed across the channel during a storm, and took possession of the dismantled fort, before morning effected a solid lodgement, and although the French cannonaded the work with field artillery all the next day, the garrison was immoveable.

Early in March a more minute survey of the general state of the defensive works was made, when it appeared that the force then assigned was quite inadequate, and that to secure it against the efforts of the enemy, twenty thousand soldiers, and a series redoubts and batteries, requiring the labour of four thousand men for three months, were absolutely necessary; and yet an unaccountable apathy prevailed. In vain did the English engineers present plans, and offer to construct works; the Spaniards would never consent to pull down a house, or destroy a garden; and had the enemy been then prepared to press onward vigorously, the city must have been lost by procrastination so fatal.

One word more for Matagorda. The capture of this place by a few intrepid men has been mentioned. Though frequently cannonaded, it had been held fifty five days, and contributed to prevent the completion of the enemy's works at the Troccadero point. This small fort, of a square form, without a ditch, with bomb-proofs insufficient for the garrison, and with one angle projecting towards the land, was little calculated for resistance; and, as it could only bring seven guns to bear, a Spanish seventy-four, and an armed flotilla, were moored on the flanks to co-operate in the defence.

The French had, however, raised great batteries behind some houses on the Troccadero, and, as day-light broke on the 21st of April, a hissing shower of heated shot falling on the seventy-four, and in the midst of the flotilla, obliged them to cut their cables and take shelter under the works of Cadiz. Then the fire of forty-eight guns and mortars of the largest size was concentrated upon the little fort of Matagorda, and the feeble parapet disappeared in a moment before this crashing flight of metal. The naked rampart, and the undaunted hearts of the garrison, remained; but the troops fell fast, the enemy shot quick and close; a staff, bearing the Spanish flag, was broken six times in an hour, and the colours were at last fastened to the angle of the work itself; while the men, especially the sailors, besought the officers to hoist the British ensign, attributing the slaughter to their fighting under a foreign flag.

Thirty hours the tempest lasted, ,and sixty-four men out of one hundred and forty were down, when General Graham sent boats to carry off the survivors. The bastion was then blown up, under the direction of Major Lefebre, an engineer of great promise; and he also fell,—the last man whose blood wetted the ruins thus abandoned.

An action must be here recorded truly heroic. A Sergeant's wife, named Retson, was in a casemate with the wounded men, when a very young drummer was ordered to fetch water from the well of the fort. Seeing the child hesitate, she snatched the vessel from his hand, braving the terrible cannonade herself; and although a shot cut the bucket-cord from her hand, she recovered the vessel, and fulfilled her mission.

In July, the British force in Cadiz was increased to eight thousand five hundred men, and Sir Richard Keats arrived to take the command of the fleet. The operations of the besiegers were thus greatly checked; and the mighty lines, constructed with so much labour and skill, led to little or nothing.

CHAPTER 13

Ciudad Rodrigo

As the spring of the year advanced, the operation of the campaign became increasingly extended and important. Reinforcements from France continued to crowd the roads. The command of these collected forces, which included seventeen thousand of the Imperial Guards, was entrusted to Massena, Prince of Essling, on account of his great name in arms. Under his auspices Ney commenced the first siege of Ciudad Rodrigo; and if he expected to carry it without delay, it only shows that, like some of his predecessors, he was liable to mistake.

The present Governor, Don Andreas Herrasti was a veteran of fifty years' service, whose silver hairs, dignified countenance, and courteous manners excited respect; and whose courage, talents, and honour were worthy of his venerable appearance. His garrison amounted to six thousand fighting men, besides the citizens; and the place, built on a height over hanging the northern bank of the Agueda river, was amply supplied with artillery and stores of all kinds. The works were, however, weak. There were no bomb-proofs, and Herrasti was obliged to place his powder in the church for security.

The country immediately about Ciudad Rodrigo, although wooded, was easy for troops, especially on the left bank of the Agueda, to which the garrison had access by a stone bridge within pistol shot of the castle-gate. But the Agueda itself rising in the Sierra de Francia, and running into the Douro, is subject to great and sudden floods; and six or seven miles below the town, near San Feliceo, the channel deepens into one continued and frightful chasm, many hundred feet deep, and overhung with huge desolate rocks.

Towards the end of April a French camp was formed, upon a lofty ridge five miles eastward of the city; and in a few days a second, and then a third arose. These portentous clouds continued to gather on the hills until June, when fifty thousand fighting men came down into the plain, and, throwing two bridges over the Agueda, begirt the fortress.

In the night of the 22nd, Julian Sanchez, with two hundred horsemen, passed silently out of the castle-gate, and, crossing the river, fell upon the nearest French posts, pierced their line in a moment, and reached the English light division then behind the Azava, six miles from Ciudad Rodrigo.

We cheerfully received the party, and three days after this, feat the batteries opened. The assailants were warmly received. Three of their magazines, by the fire of the besieged, blew up, and killed above a hundred men. On the 27th the Prince of Essling arrived in the camp, and summoned the Governor to surrender. Herrasti answered in the manner to be expected from so good a soldier; and the fire was resumed, until the 1st of July, when Massena, sensible that the mode of attack was faulty, directed the engineers to raise counter-batteries, to push on their parallels, work regularly forward, blow in the counterscarp, and pass the ditch in form.

On the 9th of July the besiegers' batteries re-opened with terrible effect. In twenty-four hours the fire of the Spanish guns was nearly silenced, part of the town was in flames, a reserve magazine exploded on the walls, the counterscarp was blown in by a mine, on an extent of thirty-six feet, the ditch filled by ruins, and a broad way made into the place. At this moment three French soldiers, suddenly running out of the ranks, mounted the breach, looked into the town, and having thus in broad day-light proved the state of affairs, discharged their muskets, and with singular success retired unhurt.

The columns of assault immediately assembled. The troops, animated by the presence of Ney, were impatient for the signal to advance. A few minutes would have sent them raging into the midst of the city; when the white flag waved on the rampart, and the venerable Governor was seen standing alone on the ruins, and signifying by his gestures that he desired to capitulate. The defence made did no discredit to the parties. Everyone lent a hand. The inhabitants contributed largely in maintaining the vigour and resolution of the garrison. Women and children, and even the blind, were earnestly engaged in providing necessaries for the fighting men. Those who were unable to bear arms encouraged those who could. Indeed, it was to the spirit of determined resistance prevailing among the people generally within the walls, that the powerful force without was so long detained there. Above forty thousand shells had been thrown into the place, and not a house remained uninjured.

CHAPTER 14

Wellington

One of the favourite designs of Napoleon at this period was to establish his power in Portugal. This the British Government was determined, if possible, to prevent; and the person selected to direct the defence of our ancient ally was Lord Wellington. Confidence was felt in no other; and it was a question whether any other military leader was in all respects properly qualified for the arduous under taking. When his Lordship required thirty thousand men for the defence of Portugal, he considered the number that could be fed rather than what was necessary to fight the enemy. On this principle he asserted that success must depend on the exertions and devotedness of the native forces.

Two points were to be secured at the very onset. One was, to concert measures by which sustenance might be secured for the united British and Portuguese army; and the other, to devise plans by which the enemy should be deprived of supplies, whenever and wherever he entered the country. In effecting this latter purpose it was demanded, (for the exactions of war are necessarily rigorous,) that the people should destroy their mills, remove their boats, break down their bridges, lay waste their fields, abandon their dwellings, and carry off their property, on whatever line the invader should penetrate; while the entire population, converted into soldiers and closing on the rear and flanks, should cut off all resources, excepting those carried in the midst of the troops. These were hard sayings; but they were dictated by stern necessity, and were positively required for the safety of the kingdom. The call was obeyed. Part of the public property was sacrificed, in order that the whole might, in some form or other, eventually be restored and rendered safe.

In pursuance of the comprehensive plans adopted by the British leader, it was necessary to find a position, covering Lisbon, where the allied forces could neither be turned by the flanks, nor forced in front by numbers, nor reduced by famine. The mountains filling the tongue of land upon which Lisbon is situated, furnished this key stone to the arch of defence. Lord Wellington then conceived the design of turning these vast mountains into one stupendous and impregnable citadel, on which to deposit the independence of the whole Peninsula. The works were forthwith commenced. Entrenchments, inundations, and redoubts, covered more than five hundred square miles of mountainous country, lying between the Tamils and the ocean.

The actual force under Lord Wellington cannot be estimated higher than eighty thousand men, while the frontier he had to defend, reckoning from Bragansa to Ayamonte, was four hundred miles long. The British forces included in the above were under thirty thousand. Every probable movement of the enemy was previously considered: at the same time the English Commander was aware how many counter-combinations were to be expected in a contest with eighty thousand French veterans, having a competent General at their head. Hence, to secure embarkation in the event of disaster, a third line of entrenchments was prepared, and twenty-four thousand tons of shipping were constantly kept in the river to receive the British forces.

CHAPTER 15

Crauford

Where all behaved so well, distinctions are unnecessary, and may appear invidious. Perhaps, however, I may be allowed to claim at least an equal share of the honours of a successful campaign for the division of the British army under the command of General Crauford, in which was included the 43rd regiment. Without attempting to institute any comparison between him and the Commander-in-chief, the comprehensiveness and strength of whose capacity in the direction of extensive movements was unrivalled, it may be safely averred, that for zeal, intrepidity of spirit, and personal prowess, Crauford was not inferior to any General of division in the forces.

His men partook in a great measure of the qualities of their leader. Inured to almost every species of warlike toil, they were formidable either for assault or defence; and never were the energies of fighting men more thoroughly tested than those of this very corps in the course of the few succeeding months.

In the midst of March, Crauford lined the banks of the Agueda with his Hussars for a distance of twenty-five miles, following the course of the river. The infantry were disposed in small parties in the villages between Almeida and the Lower Agueda. Two battalions of Portuguese Cacadores (Riflemen) soon afterwards arriving, made a total of four thousand men, and six guns. While therefore the Hussars kept a good watch at the two distant bridges, the troops could always concentrate under Almeida before the enemy could reach them on that side; and on the side of Barba del Puerco the ravine was so profound that a few companies of the 95th were considered capable of opposing any numbers.

This arrangement was suitable while the Agueda was swollen; but that river was capricious, often falling many feet in a night, without visible cause. When it was fordable, Crauford always withdrew his outposts, and concentrated his division; and his situation demanded a quickness and intelligence in his troops, the like of which has never been surpassed. Seven minutes sufficed for the division to get under arms in the middle of the night; and a quarter of an hour, night or day, to bring it in order of battle to the alarm-posts, with the baggage loaded and assembled at a convenient distance in the rear, and this not upon a concerted signal, or as a trial, but at all times, and to a certainty.

We soon found that our caution was called for. On the 19th of March General Ferey, a bold officer, attempted to surprise us, for which purpose he collected six hundred Grenadiers close to the bridge of San Felices, and just as the moon rising behind him east long shadows from the rocks, and rendered the bottom of the chasm dark, he silently passed the bridge, and, with incredible speed ascending the opposite side, bayoneted the sentries, and fell upon the piquet so fiercely, that friends and enemies went fighting into the village of Barba del Puerco, while the first shout was still echoing in the gulf below.

So sudden was the attack, and so great the confusion, that the British companies could not form, but each soldier encountering the nearest enemy, fought hand to hand; and their Colonel, Sydney Beckwith, conspicuous by his lofty stature and daring actions, a man capable of rallying a whole army in flight, urged the contest with such vigour, that in a quarter of an hour the French column was borne back, and pushed over the edge of the descent.

Soon after this the whole army was distressed for money; and Crauford, notwithstanding his prodigious activity, being unable to procure food for the division, gave the reins to his fiery temper, and seized some church plate, with a view to the purchase of corn. For this impolitic act he was immediately rebuked, and such redress granted that no mischief ensued. The proceeding itself was not, however, altogether useless, as it convinced the Priests that our distress was real.

Nothing could be more critical than our position. From the Agueda to the Coa the whole country, although studded with woods, and scooped into hollows, was free for cavalry and artillery, and there were at least six thousand horsemen and fifty guns within an hour's march of our position; and yet, trusting to his own admirable arrangements, and to the surprising discipline of his troops, Crauford still maintained his dangerous position, thus encouraging the garrison of Ciudad Rodrigo, and protecting the villages in the plain. The fall of that fortress was, however, soon announced. A Spaniard, eluding the French posts, brought a note from old Herrasti, the Governor, claiming assistance. It contained these words,—"*O venir luego! Luego! a secorrer esta plaza.*" (O come now, now, to the succour of this place!) But the gallant old man could not be relieved.

Soon after this I had the misfortune to fall into bad hands. I having had occasion to visit a neighbouring village on regimental business, and to make some small purchases for one of the officers, I was detained rather late in the evening, and on attempting on my return to cross a mountainous district without a guide, I lost my way. After wandering in various directions among rocks and low brushwood, two large dogs, singularly fierce and powerful, used by the Spaniards to protect their cattle from wolves, suddenly appeared in the attitude of springing at me. Putting on a bold front, I stepped back, and drew my bayonet, when, to my surprise, they seemed to dislike my appearance, and recoiled. Concluding that some human abode was nigh, I followed the track of the dogs, and presently arrived at an open space, where a few glowing embers indicated that a fire had recently been there.

While gazing on the spot my attention was arrested by a rushing noise quite close to my ear, and, in almost the same instant, three men darted through an adjoining copse, and were on me with incredible violence. One of them, who was armed with a halbert, made a desperate plunge with his formidable weapon; and had I not parried it, that moment would have ended my life.

The others joined in this unmanly and unaccountable attack; but though roughly used, I escaped without mortal injury. I at first imagined that the fellows were part of a banditti, living by rapine and plunder, and that, disappointed of booty, they had wreaked their resentment by violent usage. I found afterwards that they were cattle-owners; and what aggravated their conduct, a report was spread through their agency that I had a design upon their property, than which nothing was further from my thought. The outrage being reported to our Commander, Major McLeod, a Sergeant, with his piquet of men, was sent to investigate the truth.

On arriving at the place, there they found me, unable to move from the ill treatment I had received. I stated exactly what had taken place, and requested that the men might be secured, and taken to quarters, so that I might confront them before the Major. This was acceded to, and being permitted to answer for myself, I produced the proper pass, still in my possession, and soon convinced the board that I had been within the line of duty, was the only injured party, and deserved some compensation for the treatment I had received. This was immediately granted; so that with the exception of a few bruises, which grew better under the agreeable remedy just glanced at, I came off with flying colours, while the Dons paid for the entertainment.

At the beginning of July, the enemy began to appear in numbers; but, obstinate in maintaining every inch of ground, our division remained firm. The troops were marched in succession slowly, and within sight of the French, hoping that they would imagine the whole British army was come up. By this manoeuvre two days were gained, but on the 4th a strong body of the enemy assembled at Marialva; and a squadron of horse, crossing the ford below that bridge, pushed at full force towards Gallegos, driving back the piquets.

The enemy then passed the river, and the British retired, skirmishing upon Almeida, leaving two guns, a troop of British, and one of German Hussars, to cover the movement. This rear-guard drew up on a hill, half cannon-shot from a streamlet with marshy banks, which crossed the road to Almeida: in a few moments a column of French horsemen was observed coming on at a charging pace, diminishing its front as it approached the bridge, but resolute to pass, and preserving the most perfect order in spite of some well-directed shots from the guns.

Captain Krauchenberg, of the Hussars, proposed to charge: the English officer did not conceive his order warranted it, but the gallant Captain rode full speed against the head of the advanced column with his single troop, and with such a shock that he killed the leading officer, overthrew the front ranks, and drove the whole back.

This skirmish was followed by another on the 11th: on this occasion two French parties were observed, the one of infantry near Villa de Puerco, the other of cavalry at Barquillo. An open country on the right would have enabled the six squadrons to get between the infantry in Villa de Puerco and their point of retreat: this was circuitous, and Crauford preferred pushing straight through a stone enclosure as the shortest road. The enclosure proved difficult, the squadrons were separated, and the French, 200 strong, had time to draw up in a square on a rather steep rise of land; yet so far from the edge as not to be seen till the ascent was gained. The two squadrons which first arrived galloped in upon them; and the charge was rough and pushed home, but failed. The troopers received the fire of the square in front and on both sides, and in passing saw and heard the French Captain, Gauche, and his Sergeant-major, exhorting the men to shoot carefully. Meanwhile Colonel Talbot, mounting the hill with four squadrons of the 14th Dragoons, bore gallantly in upon Captain Gauche; but the latter again opened such a fire that Talbot himself and fourteen men went down close to the bayonets, and the stout Frenchman made good his retreat.

Crauford fell back to Almeida, apparently disposed to cross the Coa; yet nothing was further from his thoughts. Braving the whole French army, he had kept, with a weak division, for three months within two hours march of sixty thousand men, appropriating the resources of the plains entirely to himself. Had he been satisfied with this feat, it would have shown him to be master of some prudence; but forgetting that his stay beyond the Coa was a matter of sufferance rather than real strength, he resolved with ambition not easily excusable, in defiance of reason and the repeated order of his General, to fight again on the right bank,—a piece of rashness for which we dearly paid.

Upon a calm review of the circumstances under which this engagement took place, I consider it little short of a miracle that a single British soldier survived to describe it. The troops we had to oppose were those of a well-disciplined army, they were commanded by officers of approved talent and courage, and out-numbered us at least in the proportion of four to one. Nor, mingled as I was among the most furious combatants, can I conceive how it happened that I escaped unhurt.

CHAPTER 16

The Coa

The most dangerous crisis had now arrived: this was on the evening of the 24th of July, which was stormy, and proved to be a memorable period. Our whole force under arms consisted of four thousand infantry, eleven hundred cavalry, and six guns; and the position occupied was about one mile and a half in length, extending in an oblique line towards the Coa. The cavalry piquets were upon the plain in front, the right on some broken ground, and the left resting on an unfinished tower eight hundred yards from Almeida: the rear was on the edge of the ravine forming the channel of the Coa, and the bridge was more than a mile distant in the bottom of the chasm.

The lightning towards midnight became unusually vivid. Having been under arms for several hours, we were drenched with rain: as the day dawned a few pistol-shots in front, followed by an order for the cavalry reserve and the guns to advance, gave notice of the enemy's approach; and as the morning cleared, twenty-four thousand French infantry, five thousand cavalry, and thirty pieces of artillery were observed marching from Turones.

Our line was immediately contracted, and brought under the edge of the ravine: in an instant four thousand hostile cavalry swept the plain, and our regiment was unaccountably placed within an enclosure of solid masonry at least ten feet high, situate on the left of the road, with but one narrow outlet about half musket-shot down the ravine. While thus shut up the firing in front redoubled, the cavalry, the artillery, and the Cacadores successively passed by in retreat, and the sharp sound of the 95th Rifle was heard along the edge of the plain above. A few moments later and we should have been surrounded; but here, as in every other part of the field, the quickness and knowledge of the battalion officer remedied the faults of the General.

In little more than a minute, by united effort, we contrived to loosen some large stones, when, by a powerful exertion, we burst the enclosure, and the regiment, reformed in column of companies, was the next instant up with the Riflemen. There was no room to array the line, no time for anything but battle; every Captain carried all his company as an independent body, the whole presenting a mass of skirmishers, acting in small parties and under no regular command, yet each confident in the courage and discipline of those on his right and left, and all regulating their movements by a common discretion. Having the advantage of ground and number, the enemy broke over the edge of the ravine; their guns, ranged along the summit, played hotly with grape; and their Hussars, galloping over the glacis of Almeida, poured down the road, sabring everything in their way. The British regiments, however, extricated themselves from their perilous situation. Falling back slowly, and yet stopping and fighting whenever opportunity offered, they made their way through a rugged country, tangled with vineyards, in despite of the enemy, who was so fierce and eager, that even the horsemen rode in among the enclosures, striking at us, as we mounted the walls, or scrambled over the rocks.

Just then, I found myself within pistol-shot of the enemy, while my passage was checked by a deep chasm or ravine: as not a moment was to be lost, I contrived to mount to the edge, and, having gained the opposite side, put myself in a crouching position, and managed to slide down the steep and slippery descent without injury. On approaching the river, a more open space presented itself; but the left wing being harder pressed, and having the shortest distance, the bridge was so crowded as to be impassable: here therefore we made a stand.

The post was maintained until the enemy, gathering in great numbers, made a second burst, when the companies fell back. At this moment the right wing of the 52nd was seen marching towards the bridge, which was still crowded with the passing troops, when McLeod, a very young man, immediately turned his horse round, called to the troops to follow, and, taking off his cap, rode with a shout towards the enemy. The suddenness of the thing, and the distinguished action of the man, produced the effect he designed we all rushed after him, cheering and charging as if a whole army were behind to sustain us; the enemy's skirmishers, amazed at this unexpected movement, were directly checked.

The conflict was tremendous: thrice we repulsed the enemy at the point of the bayonet. McLeod was in the hottest of the battle, and a ball passed through the collar of his coat; still he was to be seen with a pistol in his right hand, among the last to retire. At length the bugle sounded for retreat: just then, my left-hand man, one of the stoutest in the regiment, was hit by a musket shot,—he threw his head back, and was instantly dead. I fired at the fellow who shot my comrade; and before I could reload, my pay-sergeant, Thomas, received a ball in the thigh, and earnestly implored me to carry him away. As the enemy was not far off, such a load was by no means desirable: but he was my friend; I therefore took him up; and though several shots were directed to us, they all missed, and I was able, though encumbered with such weight, to carry him safely over the bridge. At length the assistance of another soldier was procured: we then carried the wounded man between us, when he was placed on a car. He returned me sincere thanks, and, what was just then much better, gave me his canteen, out of which I was permitted to take a draught of rum: how refreshing it was, can be fully known only to myself.

As the regiments passed the bridge, they planted themselves in loose order on the side of the mountain; the artillery drew up on the summit, and the cavalry were disposed in parties on the roads to the right, because two miles higher up the stream there were fords, and beyond them the bridge of Castello Bom. The French skirmishers, swarming on the right bank, opened a biting fire, which was returned as bitterly the artillery on both sides played across the ravine, the sounds were repeated by numberless echoes; and the smoke, rising slowly, resolved itself into an immense arch, sparkling with the whirling phases of the flying shells.

The enemy despatched a Dragoon to try the depth of the stream above; but two shots from the 52nd killed man and horse, and the carcasses floating down the river discovered that it was impassable. The monotonous tones of a French drum were than heard; and in another second the head of a column was at the long narrow bridge. A drummer, and an officer in splendid uniform, leaped forward together, and the whole rushed on with loud cries. The depth of the ravine at first deceived the soldiers' aim on our side, and two-thirds of the passage were won before an English shot had brought down an enemy. A few paces onward the line of death was traced, and the whole of the leading French section fell as one man.

Still the gallant column pressed forward, but no foot could pass that terrible line: the killed and wounded rolled together, until the heap rose nearly to a level with the parapet. Our shouts now rose loudly, but they were confidently answered; and in half an hour a second column, more numerous than the first, again crowded the bridge. This time the range was better judged, and ere half the distance was passed, the multitude was again torn, shattered, dispersed, and slain: ten or twelve men only succeeded in crossing, and took shelter under the rocks at the brink of the river.

The skirmishing was renewed, and a French surgeon, coming down to the very foot of the bridge, waved his handkerchief, and commenced dressing the wounded under the hottest fire: the appeal was heard; every musket turned from him, although his still undaunted countrymen were preparing for a third attempt. This last effort was comparatively feeble, and soon failed. The combat was nevertheless continued by the French, as a point of honour to cover the escape of those who had passed the bridge, and by the English from ignorance of their object.

One of the enemy's guns was dismantled; a powder magazine blew up; and many continued to fall on both sides till four o'clock, when a heavy rain caused a momentary cessation of fire: the men among the rocks returned unmolested to their own party, the fight ceased, and we retired behind the Pinkel river. On our side upwards of three hundred were killed or wounded. The French lost more than a thousand men.

During the march that ensued, which of necessity was rapid, my mind was deeply impressed with the occurrences of the preceding eventful day. Many of my valued friends were missing, and their remains lay unburied on the spot where they fell. Colonel Hull, who had joined the regiment only the day before the action, was killed; and I afterwards saw his body, with the face downwards, thrown across the back of a mule, for conveyance to some place of interment: the Colonel's nephew was also badly wounded in the mouth, and obliged to return to England.

Despondency is not, however, the fitting mood for a soldier. Tears for the dead were soon brushed away, and, to secure our own preservation, thought was soon diverted from musing on the past, to the active operations before us. Unremitted exertions were made by the Commissariat to provide us with necessaries. Grapes were plentiful; vegetables also were within reach. Bread in sufficient quantities, with a pipe of wine in front for regimental use, afforded an agreeable prospect; and the evening after the arrival of this welcome reinforcement was spent in a good-humoured review of dangers gone by.

CHAPTER 17

On Campaign

The Captain of the company in which I served being in want of a servant, I had the honour of being engaged in that capacity: my place, however, was no sinecure, and often amounted to a rather dangerous distinction. The duties enjoined were heavy, and contributed not a little to increase the severity of general military service. When my master dismounted from his horse, I had to hold the animal, or lead him by the bridle along roads through which it was difficult to drag myself; and the horse, chafed by rough usage, and deficient feed, was frequently so restive that my employment was both irksome and laborious: this horse became an eventual favourite. Having been placed for a short time at large, he thought proper to escape, and accordingly scoured away over hill and dale, with the saddle and accoutrements of his master, including a pair of pistols in the holster, and change of clothing behind. He was observed by a party of French, who tried to secure him, but, strange to say, he was determined they should not. By a kind of instinct, to me an entire enigma, the horse chose the road in which he apparently knew his old associates were to follow; and when we had crossed the bridge, to my surprise, he was there beforehand, and waiting our arrival.

A rare and unpleasant circumstance took place here. The discipline and good order of the 43rd were proverbial: the matter was therefore so much the more vexatious. Being placed for a brief period in the vicinity of a village, the landlady of a Spanish house of entertainment had broached a puncheon of wine, which she retailed at a stipulated price. One of our men, with more wit than wisdom, got behind the cask unperceived by the lady, and having pierced the hinder end with his bayonet, drew away both for himself and friends. In an evil hour the unlucky wight was detected, and next morning was punished in presence of the regiment. That the man did wrong, is clear; but being a good soldier, and of an excellent temper withal, the event excited great regret, and the humiliating spectacle was witnessed with reluctance.

One day a bullock was killed for our use, and afforded a luxurious repast; but we were obliged to make haste about it. Scarcely had we finished; a hasty meal, when the advance of the enemy was announced. The men were unwilling to lose even a fragment of viands so scarce; and several were afterwards observed, collecting bundles of the long dry grass and making a fire, over which they frizzled pieces of meat, impaled on the end of a ramrod.

The hardships we endured in the prosecution of this retreat were increasingly severe. Personal comforts were out of the question. No change of linen could be procured; and as to a pair of stockings, the luxury was not to be thought of. As mine were worn to tatters, I contented myself without a new supply. Snatches of broken slumber were all we could obtain, though ready to stumble with weariness.

The physical energies both of myself and comrades have, since that period, often appeared wonderful, even to myself. Many a time I have marched eight or ten miles on the nourishment afforded by a little water; and even then, with a pipe and good company, we talked away dull care, and were able with three cheers to face about, and with a determined volley warn away the following foe. We were much hurt by exposure to extremes, After the exhaustion arising from a forced march, pursued for hours, during the meridian heat of this burning climate, we lay down to rest for the night; and on the following morning such was the copiousness of the fallen dew, that our blankets appeared as if dipped in water. Rising from the ground in such a condition, it will be easily imagined that our sensations were not of an enviable cast.

Even then I thought of thee, my native land; of thy rivers and vales, all so peaceful and beauteous, and they arose fairer than ever: and I thought of thee, my mother, who so often hadst cared and watched for me. But these meditations were dismissed. Had they been long indulged, my heart would have melted within me; and the time was at hand, when the sterner faculties were likely to be tried to the uttermost.

CHAPTER 18

Busaco

A sad disaster happened at this period. Almeida was besieged by Massena in person, at the head of a powerful army. The place, though regularly constructed with six bastions, ravlins, an excellent ditch and covered way, was extremely defective: with the exception of some damp casemates in one of the bastions, time was no magazine for the powder.

The garrison consisted of about four thousand men. On the 18th of July the trenches were begun; and on the morning of the 26th, the second parallel bring commenced, sixty-five pieces of artillery mounted on ten batteries threw in their fire. Many houses were soon in flames, and the garrison was unable to extinguish them; the counter fire was, however, briskly maintained, little military damage was sustained, and towards evening the cannonade slackened on both sides; but just after dark; the ground suddenly trembled, the castle burst into a thousand pieces, and gave vent to a column of smoke and fire: presently the whole town sunk into a shapeless mass of ruin.

Treason or accident had caused the magazine to explode; and the devastation was incredible. Five hundred persons were struck dead on the instant; only six houses remained standing; and the surviving garrison, aghast at the terrible commotion, disregarded all exhortations to rally. An immediate surrender was the necessary result.

The invasion of Portugal by the French now assumed a most serious aspect. Massena's command extended from the banks of the Tagus to the Bay of Biscay, and the number of his troops exceeded a hundred and ten thousand men. The view was discouraging, and was so felt by the British Ministry at home. Massena could bring sixty thousand veterans into the field, while the British force was scarcely fifty thousand, more than half of which consisted of untried men.

The Sierra Busaco was the place on which Lord Wellington fixed for his position. A succession of ascending ridges lead to this mountain, which is separated from the last by a chasm so profound, that the unassisted eye could hardly distinguish the movement of troops in the bottom. When this formidable position was chosen, some officers expressed their fears that Massena would not assail it.

"But if he do, I shall beat him," was the reply of the English leader; who was well assured that the Prince would attack.

Massena was in fact anxious for a battle, and indulged in a vision, in which he beheld the allies fly before his face. On the 22nd of September we fell back exactly a league, and encamped in a pine-wood.

One night there happened among us an extraordinary panic, for which none of us, either then or since, could assign any reasonable cause. No enemy was near, nor was any alarm given, yet suddenly large bodies of the troops started from sleep, as if seized with a frenzy, and dispersed in every direction; some climbed the trees, they knew not why: nor was there any possibility of allaying this strange terror, until some person called out that the enemy's cavalry were among them, when the soldiers mechanically fell into something like order, and the illusion instantly vanished.

On the 25th the enemy's cavalry were seen gathering in front, and the heads of three infantry columns were visible on the table-land above Mortagas, coming on abreast, and at a most impetuous pace; while heavy clouds of dust, rising and loading the atmosphere for miles behind, showed that the whole French army was in full march to attack. The cavalry skirmishers were already exchanging pistol-shots, when Lord Wellington, suddenly arriving, ordered the division to retire, and, taking the personal direction, covered the retreat with the 52nd and other troops. Nor was there a moment to lose: the enemy with great rapidity brought up both infantry and guns, and fell on so briskly, that all the skill of the General, and the readiness of the rear-guard, where I was placed, could scarcely prevent the division from being seriously engaged.

Before three o'clock, forty thousand French infantry were in position on the two points, and the sharp musketry of the skirmishers arose from the gloomy chasms beneath. The allies had now taken their stand; and along the whole of their front, skirmishers were thrown out on the mountain side, and about fifty pieces of artillery disposed upon the salient points. In the evening, in order to facilitate the approaching attack, the light French troops were observed stealing by twos and threes into the lowest parts of the valley, endeavouring to make their way up the wooded dells and hollows, and to establish themselves unseen, close to the piquets of the light division. Some companies of Rifle corps and Cacadores checked this; but similar attempts made with more or less success, at different points of the position, seemed to indicate a night attack, and excited all the vigilance of the troops. Had it not been so, none but veterans tired of war could have slept. The weather was calm and fine, and the dark mountain masses rising on either side were crowned with innumerable watch-fires, around which, more than a hundred thousand brave men were gathered.

The attack began on the following morning before daybreak. Three columns were led by Ney, and two by Reynier, the points being about three miles asunder. The resistance was spirited, and six guns played along the slope with grape; but in less than half an hour the French were close upon the summit, so swiftly did they scale the mountain, overthrowing every thing that opposed their progress. The leading battalions immediately established themselves upon the higher rocks, and a confused mass wheeled to the right, intending to sweep the summit of the sierra; but at that moment Lord Wellington directed two guns to open with grape upon their flank, while a heavy musketry was poured into their front; and in a little time the 45th and 88th regiments charged so furiously that even fresh men could not have withstood them.

The French, quite spent with their previous exertion, opened a straggling fire, and both parties, mingling together, went down the mountain side with mighty clamour and confusion; the dead and dying strewing the way, even to the bottom of the valley. Meanwhile the French who had first gained the summit had re-formed their ranks, with the right resting upon a precipice overhanging the reverse side of the sierra; and thus the position was in fact gained, if any reserve had been at hand; but just then General Leith, who saw what had taken place, came on rapidly.

Keeping the Royals in reserve, he directed the 38th to turn the right of the French; but the precipice prevented this; and meanwhile Colonel Cameron, informed by a staff officer of the critical state of affairs, formed the 9th regiment in line under a violent fire, and, without returning a single shot, ran in upon and drove the Grenadiers from the rocks with irresistible bravery, and yet with excellent discipline; refraining from pursuit, lest the crest of the position should be again lost, for the mountain was so rugged that it was impossible to judge clearly of the general state of the action.

On that side, however, the victory was secure. Ney's attack was equally unsuccessful. From the abutment of the mountain on which be discerned. The table-land was sufficiently hollow to conceal the 43rd and 52nd regiments, drawn up in a line; and a quarter of a mile behind them, but on higher ground, and close to the convent, a brigade of German infantry appeared to be the only solid line of resistance on this part of the position. In front of the two British regiments, some rocks over-hanging the descent furnished natural embrasures, in which the guns of the division were placed, and the whole face of the hill was planted with the skirmishers of the Rifle corps, and of the two Portuguese Cacadore battalions.

While it was yet dark, on listening attentively, we heard a straggling musketry in the deep hollows separating the armies; and when the light broke, the three divisions of the 6th corps were observed entering the woods below, and throwing forward a profusion of skirmishers soon afterwards. The French ascended with wonderful cheerfulness, and though the light troops plied them unceasingly with musketry, and the artillery bullets swept through their ranks, the order of advance was never disturbed. Ross's guns were worked with incredible swiftness, yet their range was contracted every round, and the enemy's shot came singing up in a sharper key, until the skirmishers, breathless, and begrimed with powder, rushed over the edge of the ascent, when the artillery suddenly drew back, and the victorious cries of the French were heard within a few yards of the summit.

Crauford, who, standing alone on one of the rocks, had been intently watching the progress of the attack, then turned, and in a quick shrill tone desired the two regiments in reserve to charge. The next moment eighteen hundred British bayonets went over the hill. Our shouts startled the French column; and yet so truly brave were the hostile leaders, that each man of the first section raised his musket, and two officers and ten men fell before them, so unerring was their aim. They could do no more: we were on them with resistless impetuosity. The head of their column was violently overturned, and driven upon the rear; both flanks were lapped over by our wings; and three terrible discharges at five yards distance completed the rout. In a few minutes a long line of carcasses and broken arms indicated the line of retreat.

The main body of the British stood fast, but several Companies followed in pursuit down the mountain. Before two o'clock, Crauford having assented to a momentary truce, parties of both armies were mixed amicably together, searching for the wounded men. Towards evening, however, a French company having impudently seized a village within half musket-shot of our division, and refusing to retire, it so incensed Crauford, that, turning twelve guns on the village, he overwhelmed it with bullets for half an hour. A company of the 43rd was then sent down, who cleared the place in a few minutes.

An affecting incident, contrasting strongly with the savage character of the preceding events, added to the interest of the day. A poor orphan Portuguese girl, about seventeen years of age, and very handsome, was seen coming down the mountain, and driving an ass loaded with all her property through the midst of the French army. She had abandoned her dwelling in obedience to the proclamation; and now passed over the field of battle with simplicity which told she was unconscious of her perilous situation, and scarcely understanding which were the hostile and which the friendly troops, for no man on either side was so brutal as to molest her.

In this battle of Busaco, the French, after astonishing acts of valour, were repulsed. General Graindorge, and about eight hundred men, were slain, beside nearly five thousand wounded; while the loss of the allies did not exceed thirteen hundred. After this trial, Massena judged the position of Busaco impregnable, and to turn it by the Mondego impossible, as the allies could pass that river quicker than himself. But a peasant informed him of the road leading from Mortagas to Boyalva, and he resolved to turn Lord Wellington's left. To cover this movement the skirmishing was renewed with such vigour on the 28th, that many thought a general battle would take place; and yet the disappearance of baggage and the throwing up of entrenchments on the hill, covering the roads to Mortagas, indicated some other design. It was not till evening, when the enemy's masses in front being sensibly diminished, and his cavalry descried winding over the distant mountains, that the project became quite apparent.

CHAPTER 19
Coimbra

On the 1st of October, our outposts were attacked but the French, on entering the plain of Coimbra, suffered some loss from a cannonade; and the British cavalry were drawn up in line, but with no serious intention of fighting, and were soon after withdrawn across the Mondego. The light division then marched hastily to gain the defiles of Condeixa, which commences at the end of the bridge. At this juncture all the inhabitants of the place rushed simultaneously out, who had not before quitted the place, each with what could be caught up in the hand, and driving before them a number of animals loaded with sick people or children.

At the entrance to the bridge the press was so great that the troops halted for a few moments, just under the prison. The jailer had fled with the keys; the prisoners, crowding to the windows, were endeavouring to tear down the bars with their hands, and even with their teeth; some were shouting in the most frantic manner, while the bitter lamentations of the multitude increased, and the pistol-shots of the cavalry, engaged at the fords below, were distinctly heard.

Captain William Campbell burst the prison doors, and released the wretched inmates, while the troops forced their way over the bridge; yet, at the other end, the up-hill road, passing between high rocks, was so crowded, that no effort, even of the artillery, could make way. At last some of the infantry opened a passage on the right flank, and by great exertions the road was cleared for the guns; but it was not until after dusk that the division reached Condeixa, although the distance was less than eight miles. Hitherto the marches had been easy, the weather fine, and provisions abundant; nevertheless, the usual mischievous disorders of a retreat had shown themselves. In Coimbra, a quantity of harness and entrenching tools lay scattered in the streets; at Leiria, the magazines were plundered by the troops and camp followers; and at Condeixa a magazine of tents, shoes, spirits, and salt meat was destroyed, or abandoned to the enemy; and the streets were flowing ankle-deep with wasted rum, while the Portuguese division, only a quarter of a mile distant, could receive only half the usual supply of liquor.

It is with some regret I reflect, that at this period, though exposed to dangers so imminent, I was carried away in some degree with the torrent of prevailing dissipation. Not that during any period of my active service I ever suffered the pleasure of conviviality, so called, to interfere with my duty. I was indeed often astonished to notice the reckless gaiety of my companions in arms, many of whom would crowd around the evening card-table, though aware that by dawn of day they might be engaged in mortal combat. In the midst of examples so contaminating, certain principles of morality, aided perhaps by a little natural gravity, were never totally subverted; and, under the blessing of God, preserved me from the grosser vices. Insensible and ungrateful indeed I must have been not to have perceived and felt the mercies of divine Providence; for during the entire period of my active service, though exposed to perils almost unnumbered, I was not only preserved alive, but had been exempted from sickness, and therefore able, without a single exception, to maintain my place in the division.

Massena resumed his march on the 4th. Leaving his sick and wounded with a slender guard at Coimbra, amounting altogether to four thousand seven hundred men, he resumed his march by Condeixa and Leiria. His hospital was established at the Convent of Santa Clara, on the left bank of the river; and all the inhabitants who were unable to reach the lines, came down from their hiding-places in the mountains. But scarcely had the Prince left the city, when Trant, Miller, and Wilson, with nearly ten thousand militia, closed upon his rear, occupying the sierras on both sides the Mondego, and cutting off all communication with Almeida. The English army retreated; the right by Thomar and Santarem, the centre by Batalha and Rio Mayor, the left by Olobaca and Obidos; and at the same time a native force under Colonel Blunt was thrown into Peniché.

Massena followed in one column, by the way of Rio Mayor; but mean while a capital exploit, performed by a partisan officer, convicted the Prince of bad generalship, and shook his plan of invasion to the base.

Colonel Trant reached Milheada, and, believing that his arrival was unknown at Coimbra, he resolved to attack the French in that city. Having surprised a small post at Fornos, early in the morning of the 7th, he sent his cavalry at full gallop through the streets of Coimbra, with orders to pass the bridge, and cut off all communications with the French army. Mean time his infantry penetrated at different points into the principal parts of the town; and the enemy, astounded, made little or no resistance. The convent of St. Clara surrendered at discretion; and thus, on the third day after the Prince of Essling had quitted the Moudego, his depots and hospitals, with nearly five thousand prisoners, wounded and unwounded, among which there was a company of the marines of the Imperial Guard, fell into the hands of a small militia force. But Crauford, who had reached Alemguer on the 9th, was still there at three o'clock on the afternoon of the 10th.

The weather being stormy, we were placed under cover, and no indication of marching was given. The cavalry had already filed into the lines; yet no guards were posted, no patrols sent forward, nor any precautions taken against surprise, although the town, situated in a deep ravine, was peculiarly favourable for such an attempt.

It was clear to me, and others, that our officers were uneasy at this posture of affairs; the height in front was anxiously watched, and about four o'clock some French Dragoons on the summit were observed. The alarm was given, and the regiments got under arms; but the posts of assembly had been marked on an open space very much exposed, and from whence the road led through an ancient gateway to the top of the mountain behind. The enemy's numbers increased every moment, and they endeavoured to create a belief that their, artillery was come up: this feint was easily seen through, but the, General desired the regiments to break, and reform on the other side of the archway, out of gun-range; and immediately all was disorder.

The baggage animals were still loading, the streets were crowded with the followers of the division, and the whole in one confused mass rushed or were driven headlong to the archway. Several were crushed, and with worse troops general panic must have ensued; but the greater number of the soldiers, ashamed of; the order, stood firm in their ranks until the confusion abated. Nevertheless the mischief was sufficiently great; and the enemy's infantry, descending the heights, endeavoured, some to turn the town on the left, while others pushed directly through the streets in pursuit; and thus, with our front in disorder, and our rear skirmishing, the retreat was commenced. The weather was, however, so boisterous that the firing soon ceased, and a few wounded, with the loss of some baggage, was all the hurt sustained.

I was on this occasion on the verge of considerable personal danger. Having been ordered by an officer to procure forage for his horse, I incautiously ventured too near the enemy; and being further tempted by some clusters of fine grapes, accidentally noticed, I remained some little time to discuss them. On a sudden I found that the last column of the British was out of sight, while imperceptibly to myself the advanced horsemen of the French had nearly hemmed me in. Fully aware of my danger, which I felt conscious had been increased by my agreeable but untimely repast, I was aroused to instant exertion, and was happy enough to elude surrounding scouts and reach my division. Having, however, exceeded my commission, by taking care of myself as well as the horse, and exposed both to extreme jeopardy, I was glad to resign the animal to his owner, and resume my musket and place in the ranks with out notice: and had no objection to perceive that my error had been unnoticed both by foes and friends.

The Captain of the company in whose service I had engaged myself, like many others, had not much time to spare. When an alarm was given of the enemy's approach, we were preparing for dinner. Three or four officers messed together; and on that day another or two were expected, by way of a small party. Culinary preparations on a moderate scale were going on, and I had just opened the Captain's trunk, and taken out some table-linen, when, lo! the well-known bugle sounded to arms. Aware that something unexpected had happened, I ran up stairs, and on looking out at a back window, I saw the enemy on the brow of a mountain, a column of whom were rapidly descending into the town.

Coming down in haste, I found the dinner ready; but there is many a slip between the nip and the lip; and, reaching across the table, which was ready garnished, I swept the whole—utensils, food, and all–into the orifice of a large travelling-bag, and made my way with it into the street. Confusion and disorder are terms too weak to describe the condition of the public thoroughfare. This time, thought I, we shall be surely taken. The Captain clamoured for his horse: I was as urgent for a mule to carry the baggage: every minute of delay seemed an hour. At length, by uncommon effort, we cleared, the town, and though the roads were bad, reached a small village, within the lines, before midnight. I was billeted, with several officers, in a gentleman's house: it was well furnished; but I regret, to add, that in a few days most of the moveables were destroyed: the proprietor, it would appear, had a presentiment of approaching, injury; for previous to our actual entrance on the premises, he and his family had decamped.

CHAPTER 20

The Lines of Torres Vedras

I have already made some allusion to the lines of Torres Vedras, thrown up for the defence of Lisbon by Lord Wellington. These lines consisted of three distinct ranges of defence. The first, extending from Alhandra on the Tagus to the mouth of the Zizandre on the sea-coast, was, following the inflections of the hills, twenty-nine miles long. The second, traced at a distance varying from six to ten miles in rear of the first, stretched from Quintella, on the Tagus, to the mouth of the St. Lorenzo, being twenty-four miles in length. The third, intended to cover a forced embarkation, should it become necessary, extended from Passo d'Arcos, on the Tagus, to the tower of Junquera, on the coast. Here an outer line, constructed on an opening of three thousand yards, enclosed an entrenched camp, designed to cover the embarkation with fewer troops, should the operation be delayed by bad weather: and within this second camp, Fort St. Julian's, whose high ramparts and deep ditches defied an escalade, was armed and strengthened to enable a rear-guard to protect both itself and the army.

Of these stupendous lines, the second, whether regarded for its strength or importance, was the principal, and the others only appendages; the one as a final place of refuge, the other as an advanced work to stem the violence of the enemy, and to enable the army to take up its ground on the second line without hurry or pressure. The aim and scope of all the works were to bar those passes, and to strengthen the favourable fighting positions between them, without impeding the movements of the army. The fortifications extended to the space of fifty miles: there were one hundred and fifty forts, and not fewer than six hundred pieces of artillery mounted within them, while the river was protected by gun-boats manned with British marines.

Massena was astonished at the extent and strength of works, the existence of which had only become known to him five days before he came upon them. He employed several days in examining their nature, and was as much at a loss at the end of his inspection as at the beginning. The heights of Alhandra he judged unattackable; but the valleys of Calandrix and Aruda attracted his attention.

There were here frequent skirmishes with the light division to oblige Crauford to show his force; but by making Aruda an advanced post, he rendered it impossible to discover his true position without a serious affair; and in a short time the division, with prodigious labour, secured the position, in a manner which was spoken of with admiration.

Across the ravine on the left, a loose stone wall, sixteen feet thick, and forty feet high, was raised: and across the great valley of Aruda, a double line of abatis was drawn; not composed, as is usual, of the limbs of trees, but of full grown oaks and chestnuts, dug up with all their roots and branches, dragged by main force for several hundred yards, and then reset and crossed, so that no human strength could break through. Breast-works at convenient distances, to defend this line of trees, were then cast up; and along the summit of the mountain, for the space of nearly three miles, including the salient points, other stone walls, six feet high, and four in thickness, with banquettes, were built, so that a good defence might have been made against the attacks of twenty thousand men.

The increased strength of the works in general soon convinced Massena that it was impracticable to force the lines without great reinforcements; and towards the end of October the hospitals, stores, and other encumbrances of the French army, were removed to Santarem.

On the 31st of the month two thousand men forded the Zezere above Punheta, to cover the construction of a bridge; and a remarkable exploit was performed by a Sergeant of the 16th Dragoons, named Baxter. This man, having only five troopers, came suddenly upon a piquet of fifty men, who were cooking. The Frenchmen ran to their arms, and killed one of the Dragoons; but the rest broke in amongst them so strongly, that Baxter with the assistance of some countrymen, made forty-two captives.

On the 19th the light division entered the plain between the Rio-Mayor and the Tagus, and advanced against the heights by a sedgy marsh. The columns on our side were formed for attack and the skirmishers of the light division were exchanging shots' with the enemy when it was found that the guns belonging to Pack's brigade had not arrived; and Lord Wellington, not quite, satisfied with the appearance of his adversary's force, after three hours' demonstrations, ordered the troops to retire to their former; ground. It was indeed evident that the French were resolved to maintain their position. Every advantageous spot of ground was fully occupied, the most advanced sentinels boldly returned the fire of the skirmishers, large bodies of reserve were descried, some in arms, others cooking; the strokes of the hatchet, and the fall of trees, resounded from the woods upon the hills; and the commencement of a triple line of abatis, and the fresh earth of entrenchments, were discernible in many places.

Our active light division was, however, again in motion. General Crauford thought that the hostile troops who had shown themselves, amounted merely to a rear-guard of the enemy. His eager spirit could not bear to be restrained; and seizing a musket, he advanced in the night along the cause-way, followed only by a Sergeant, and commenced a personal skirmish with the French piquets, from whose fire he escaped by miracle, convinced at last that the enemy were not in flight.

Lord Wellington judged it best to remain on the defensive, and strengthen the lines. With this view the light division, supported by a brigade of cavalry, occupied Valle, and the heights overlooking the marsh and inundation; the bridge at the end of the causeway was mined; a sugar-loaf shaped hill, looking straight down the approach, was crowned with embrasures for artillery, and laced in front with a zig-zag covered way, capable of containing five hundred infantry. Thus the causeway being blocked, the French could not, while the inundation was maintained, make any sudden irruption from Santarem.

About this period, a column of French, six thousand strong, scoured all the country beyond the Zezere, and contrived to secrete a quantity of food near Pedragoa, while other detachments arriving on the Mondego, below Coimbra, even passed that river, and carried off four hundred oxen and two thousand sheep intended for the allies. These excursions gave rise to horrible excesses, which broke down the discipline of the French army, and were not always executed with impunity. The British cavalry at various times redeemed many cattle, and brought in a considerable number of prisoners.

Finding the drudgery of servitude, when added to my customary military duty, greater than I could well sustain, I requested permission to resign my situation with the Captain; and we parted, mutually satisfied with past acquaintance, and on the fairest terms. While in the vicinity of Santarem, the unarmed French and English soldiers, while procuring wine for the respective forces, were frequently intermingled in the same cellar, when there seemed to exist a tacit understanding that all animosity was suspended. The liquor was, however, sometimes too powerful; and one of our men who had been a good soldier, after a sad debauch, relapsed into a lit of despondency: the inordinate cup was then resorted to, but is usual, it lifted him up, only to throw him into lower depths of misery. He then deserted; and when taken, seized an opportunity of placing the muzzle of a musket to his mouth, and setting his foot upon the trigger, blew his head to atoms.

The French in their retreat from Santarem, had either consumed or destroyed every particle of food that came within their reach, so that the country was a spacious desert. During a sharp day's march in pursuit, a horrible calamity was unexpectedly disclosed. While passing over a desolate mountain, a large house standing alone, and apparently deserted, was discovered near the line of our route. Prompted by curiosity, several men turned aside to inspect the interior, where they found a number of famished wretches crowded together, for no other conceivable purpose but to die in company. Thirty women and children had perished for want of food, and lay dead upon the floor; while about half that number of survivors sat watching the remains of those who had fallen. Of those who thus perished the bodies were not much emaciated, but the muscles of the face were invariably drawn transversely, giving the appearance of a smile, and presenting the most ghastly sight imaginable. Most of the living were unable to move; and it had been by great exertion that they had crawled to a little distance from the group of death. The soldiers offered some refreshment to these unfortunate persons; but one man only had sufficient strength to eat. The women seemed patient and resigned, and even-in this distress had arranged the bodies of those who first died with decency and care.

CHAPTER 21

Affairs in the South

The blockade of Cadiz was now prosecuted with unusual vigour by the French forces. The chain of forts they had built was perfected. The batteries at the Trocaderos were powerful, and the flotillas ready for action. Soult repaired in person to San Luear; and in the last night of October thirty pinnaces and gun-boats slipped out of the Guadalquivir, eluded the allied fleet, passed along the coast to Rota, and from thence, aided by shore-batteries, fought their way to Santa-Maria and the San-Pedro.

The flotilla was afterwards transported over-land; and in the ensuing month one hundred and thirty armed vessels and transports were assembled in the Trocadero canal. At that celebrated point there were immense batteries, and some notable pieces of ordnance, called cannon-mortars, or Villantroys, after the inventor. These huge engines were east in Seville, and, being placed in slings, threw shells with such prodigious force as to range over Cadiz, a distance of more than five thousand yards; but to obtain this flight, the shells were partly filled with lead, so that the charge of powder was proportionately of less effective explosion.

While Cadiz was thus begirt, a furious engagement took place at Cerra de Puereo, called by the English the heights of Barossa, about four miles from the sea-mouth of the Santa-Petri. Barossa is a low ridge creeping in from the coast about a mile and a half, and overlooking a high and broken plain of small extent. Graham, who commanded the British, was extremely desirous of holding the Barossa height, as the key both to offensive and defensive movements.

Our Spanish allies on this occasion behaved scandalously; indeed nothing but the unflinching firmness and courage of the English troops could have saved the army from entire ruin. Major Brown, seeing the general confusion arising from the defeat of the Spaniards, and being unable to stem the torrent, slowly retired into the plain, sending notice of what was passing to Graham, and demanding orders. That General, being then near Bermeja, answered that he was to fight; and instantly facing about himself, regained the plains with the greatest celerity, when, to his surprise, he beheld the Spanish rear-guard and baggage flying in confusion, the French cavalry between the summit and the sea, and Laval close on his own left flank.

In this desperate situation he felt that to retreat upon Bermeja, and thus bring the enemy pell-mell with the allies on that narrow bridge, must be disastrous: hence, without a moment's hesitation, he resolved to attack, although the key of the field of battle was already in the enemy's possession.

Ten guns, under Major Duncan, instantly opened a terrific fire against Laval's column, while Colonel Barnard, with the Riflemen, and the Portuguese companies, running out to the left, commenced the right. The remainder of the British troops, without any attention to regiments or brigades, so sudden was the affair, formed two masses, one of which, under General Dukes, marched hastily against Ruffin, and the other, under Colonel Wheatley, against Laval. Duncan's guns ravaged the French ranks; Laval's artillery replied with spirit; Ruffin's batteries took Wheatley's columns in flank; and the infantry on both sides pressed forward eagerly and with a pealing musketry; but when near together, a fierce, rapid, prolonged charge of the British overthrew the first line of the French, and, notwithstanding its extreme valour, drove it in confusion over a narrow dip of ground upon the second, which was almost immediately broken in the same manner, and only the chosen battalion, hitherto posted on the right, remained to cover the retreat.

Meanwhile Brown, receiving his orders, had marched headlong against Ruffin. Nearly half of his detachment went down under the enemy's last fire; yet he maintained the fight until Dilkes's column, which had crossed a deep hollow and never stopped even to re-form the regiments, came up, with little order indeed, but in a fierce mood, when the whole ran up towards the summit.

There was no slackness on any side, and at the very edge of the ascent their opponents met them. A dreadful, and for some time a doubtful fight ensued. Ruffin and Chaudron Rousseau, commanding the chosen Grenadiers, both fell, mortally wounded. The English bore strongly onward; and their incessant slaughtering fire forced the French from the hill, with the loss of three guns and many brave men. The defeated divisions retired concentrically, and having soon met, they endeavoured with great energy to re-form and renew the action; but the fire of Duncan's guns, close, rapid ,and destructive, rendered the attempt vain. Victor was soon in full retreat; and the British, having been twenty-four hours under arms, were too exhausted to pursue.

In this brief but desperate fight upwards of twelve hundred British soldiers, and more than two thousand Frenchmen were killed or wounded: from the latter, six; guns, an eagle, and two Generals, both mortally wounded, were taken, together with four hundred other prisoners.

CHAPTER 22

Redhina

The activities of this spirited campaign were maintained in other places. Badajos was sorely pressed by the French. Early in March, the second parallel being completed, and the Pardaleras taken into the works, the approaches were carried by sap to the covered way; mines were also prepared to blow in the counterscarp; and yet Rafael Menacho, the Governor, was not dismayed: his sallies were frequent and vigorous; he constructed new entrenchments where necessary; and every thing went on prosperously till the evening of the 2nd, when in a sally, in which the nearest French batteries were carried, the guns spiked, and trenches partly ruined, Menacho was killed, and the command fell to Imas, a man so unworthy that a worse could not be found. At once the spirit of the garrison died away; for cowardice is often contagious: the besiegers' works rapidly advanced, the ditch was passed, a lodgement was made on one of the ravlins, the rampart was breached, and, the fire of the besieged being nearly silenced, on the 10th of March the place was summoned in a peremptory manner: not that there was the least need to surrender.

A strong body of British and Portuguese were in full march for the relief of the place: this information had been communicated by telegraph; besides which Imas had been informed by a confidential messenger, that Massena was in full retreat. The breach was not practicable, provisions were plentiful, the garrison above eight thousand strong; the French army reduced by sickness and the previous operations to fewer than fourteen thousand men. Imas, how ever, instantly surrendered; but he also demanded that his Grenadiers should march out of the breach: this was granted, and he was obliged to enlarge the opening before they could do so. Yet this man, so overwhelmed with opprobrium, was never punished.

Massena continued to retreat; and a skirmish, attended with some loss on both sides, unexpectedly took place at Pombal. The Commander just named was so closely followed by our division, that, the streets being still encumbered, Ney drew up a rear-guard on a height behind the town, and threw a detachment into the old castle. He had, however, waited too long: the French army was moving in some confusion, and in an extended column of march, by a narrow defile between the mountains and the Soire river, which was fordable; while the British divisions were in rapid motion on the left bank, with the design of crossing lower down, and cutting Massena's line of retreat; but darkness came on, and the operation terminated in a sharp conflict at Pombal, whence the 95th and the 3rd Cacadores drove the French from the castle and town with such vigour, that the latter could not destroy the bridge, though it was mined for the purpose.

Daybreak on the 12th saw both armies in movement; and eight miles of march brought the head of the British into a hollow way leading to a high table-land, on which Ney had disposed five thousand infantry, a few squadrons of cavalry, and some light guns. His centre was opposite to the hollow road; his wings were covered by the woody heights which he occupied with light troops. Behind him arose the village of Redhina, situated on low ground; in front of which were posted a division of infantry, a regiment of cavalry, and a battery of heavy guns, all so skilfully disposed as to give the appearance of considerable force.

After examining the enemy's position for a short time, Lord Wellington first directed the light division to attack the wooded slopes covering Ney's right; and in less than an hour these orders were executed. The woods were presently cleared, and our skirmishers advanced even to the open plain beyond: just then, the French battalions, supported by four guns, opened a heavy rolling fire, and at the same moment, Colonel Farriere, of the 3rd French Hussars, charged and took fourteen prisoners. This officer, during the whole campaign, had never failed to break in upon the skirmishers in the most critical moments; sometimes with a squadron, sometimes with only a few men: he was, however, sure to be found in the right place.

The British light division, commanded by Sir William Erskine, consisted of five battalions of infantry, and six guns, and was formed so that it out-flanked the French right. It was also reinforced with two regiments of Dragoons: meanwhile Picton seized the woody heights protecting the French left, and thus Ney's position was exposed. Nevertheless, that Marshal, observing that Lord Wellington, deceived as to his real numbers, was bringing the mass of the allied troops into line, far from re treating, even charged Picton's skirmishers, and continued to hold his ground with astonishing confidence.

In this posture both sides remained for about an hour, when three shots were fired from the British centre as a signal for a forward movement, and a most splendid spectacle of war was exhibited. The woods seemed alive with troops, and in a few moments thirty thousand men, forming three gorgeous lines of battle, were stretched across the plain; but bending on a gentle curve, and moving majestically forward, while horsemen and guns springing simultaneously onward from the centre and left wing, charged under a volley from the French battalions: the latter were instantly hidden by the smoke; and when that cleared away, no enemy was to be seen. Ney keenly watched the progress of this grand formation, and having opposed Picton's foremost skirmishers with his left, withdrew the rest of his people with such rapidity that he gained the village before the cavalry could touch him: the utmost efforts of Picton's skirmishers and of the horse artillery scarcely enabled them to gall the hind most of the French. One howitzer was, indeed, dismounted close to the bridge, but the village of Redhina was in flames. The Marshal was hard pressed, for the British were thundering at his rear; and the light troops of the 3d division, chasing like heated blood-hounds, passed the river almost at the same time with the French: Ney, at length, fell back upon the main body at Condeixa. The mind is sometimes impressed by trifling occurrences, especially when they take place un-expectedly, or are at all out of the common way.

I remember that in the midst of the clangor and firing just described, a hare emerged from the woods, and for some time amused herself by sundry doubles and evolutions be-tween the hostile lines at length, as if satisfied that enough had been seen, she suddenly disappeared. The other event is, that the tallest man I ever saw had been a private in the French ranks at Redhina: he was lying dead on the road side. Our forces continued to drive the enemy. Massena, in repair-ing to Fonte-Coberta, had left orders to fire Condeixa at a certain hour: these gentlemen left nothing willingly behind them, hut ruin and desolation. In a few days we came up with the rear. Picton contrived to wind round the bluff side of a mountain about right miles distant: as he was already be-yond the French left, instant confusion pervaded their camp. The British immediately pushed forward; their advance was extremely rapid, and it is affirmed that the Prince of Essling, who was on the road, only escaped capture by taking the feathers out of his hat, and riding through some of the light troops. Condeixa being thus evacuated, the British cavalry pushed towards Coimbra, and cutting off Montbrun, cap-tured part of his horsemen.

The rest of the army kindled their fires, and the light division, in which, as usual, I was stationed, planted piquets close up to the enemy; but about ten at night the French divisions, whose presence was unknown to Lord Wellington, stole out, and passing along the front of the British posts, made for Miranda de Corvo.

CHAPTER 23

Santarem

The noise of their march was heard, but the night was dark it was imagined to be the moving of the French to the rear, and being so reported to Sir William Erskine, that officer put the light division in march at day-light on the 14th: our movements partook of extraordinary rashness; and what increased the danger, we were insensible of it.

The morning was so obscured that nothing could be distinguished at the distance of a hundred feet, but the sound of a great multitude was heard on the hills in front, and it being evident that the French were there in force, many officers represented the impropriety of thus advancing without orders, and in such a fog: but Erskine, with what is deemed astounding negligence, sent the 52nd forward in a simple column of sections, without a vanguard or other precaution, and even before the piquets had come in from their posts. The road dipped suddenly, descending into a valley, and the regiment was immediately lost in the mist, which was so thick that the troops, unconsciously passing the enemy's outposts, had nearly captured Ney himself, whose bivouac was close to the piquets.

The riflemen followed in a few moments, and the rest of the division was about to plunge into the same gulf, when the rattling of musketry, and the booming of round shot was heard; and when the vapour slowly rose, the 52nd were seen on the slop of the opposite mountain engaged, without support, in the midst of the enemy's army. At this moment Lord Wellington arrived, an the whole of the light division were pushed forward to sustain the 52nd.

The enemy's ground was so extensive, and his skirmishers s thick and so easily supported, that in a little time the division was necessarily stretched out in one thin thread, and closely engaged in every part without any reserve; nor could it even thus present an equal front, until Picton sent the Riflemen of the 60th to prolong the line.

The fight was vigorously maintained amidst the numerous stone enclosures on the mountain-side; some advantages were gained, and the right of the enemy was partially turned, yet the main position could not be shaken until Picton and Cole had turned it by the left. Ney then commenced his retreat, retiring from ridge to ridge with admirable precision, and for a long time without confusion and with very little loss. Towards the middle of the day, however, the British guns and the skirmishers got within range of his masses, and the retreat became more rapid and less orderly; yet he finally gained the strong pass of Miranda de Corvo, which was secured by the main body of the French. The loss in the light division this day was eleven officers and a hundred and fifty men, and about a hundred prisoners were taken.

On the 15th the weather was so obscure that the allies could not reach the Ceira before four o'clock in the afternoon, and the troops as they came up proceeded to kindle fires for the night. The French right rested on some thick and wooded ground, and their left on the village of Fons d'Aronce; but Lord Wellington, having cast a rapid glance over it, directed the light division, who were seldom forgotten when honour was to be obtained, to hold the right in play, and at the same moment the horse artillery, galloping forward to a rising ground, opened with great and sudden effect. Ney's left wing, being surprised and overthrown by

the first charge, dispersed in a panic, and fled in such confusion towards the river that some, missing the fords, were
drowned, and others, crowding on the bridge, were crushed
to death.

On the right the ground was so rugged and close that the
action resolved itself into a skirmish; and thus Ney was able
to use some battalions to check the pursuit of his left; but
meanwhile darkness came on, and the French troops in their
disorder fired upon each other. Only four officers and sixty
men fell on the side of the British: the enemy's loss was not
less than five hundred, of which one half were drowned; and
an eagle was afterwards found in the bed of the river when
the waters had subsided.

Ney maintained the left bank of the Ceira until every encumbrance had passed, and then, blowing up seventy feet of
the bridge, sent his corps on. Thus terminated the first part
of the retreat from Santarem, in which, though the ability of
the French Commander was conspicuous, it revealed much
that savoured of, a harsh and ruthless spirit. Almost every
horror that could make war hideous attended this dreadful
march. Death was dealt out in all modes. Unpitying vengeance seemed to steel every breast, lives were lost by wounds,
by fatigue, by fire, by water, besides the numerous victims
of famine.

One of my comrades going out at dusk in search of provisions, on turning a corner stumbled over the body of a
recently murdered man. The natives were of course excited
to retaliate, and Colonel Napier once saw a peasant cheering
on his dog to devour the dead and dying; the spirit of cruelty
once unchained, smote even the brute creation.

On the 15th, the French General, in order to diminish the
encumbrances on his march, ordered a number of beasts of
burden to be destroyed. The inhuman fellow charged with
the execution, who, if known, would have long since been
hooted from society, ham-stringed five hundred asses, and

left them to starve; and thus they were found by the British army. The acute, but deep expression of pain, visible in these poor creatures' looks, wonderfully aroused the fury of the soldiers; and so little weight has reason with the multitude, when opposed by momentary sensation, that had prisoners been taken at that moment, no quarter most assuredly would have been given.

CHAPTER 24
Sabugal

At day-light on the 3rd of April our nearness to the enemy indicated the approach of another collision. The English General, having ten thousand men pivoted on the 5th division at Sabugal, designed to turn Reynier's left, and surround him before he could be succoured. This well-concerted plan was marred by one of those accidents to which war is always liable, and brought on the combat of Sabugal, one of the hottest in which I was ever engaged. The morning was so foggy that the troops could not gain their respective posts of attack with that simultaneous regularity which is so essential to success.

Colonel Beckwith, who commanded the first brigade, halted at a ford to await orders, and at that moment a staff officer rode up, and somewhat hastily asked why he did not attack. The thing appeared rash; but with an enemy in front he could make no reply; and instantly passing the river, which was deep and rapid, mounted a steep wooded hill on the other side. Many of the men were up to their middle in water; and a dark heavy rain coming on, it was impossible for some time to distinguish friends from foes. The attack was thus made too soon; for owing to the obscurity, none of the divisions of the army had reached their respective posts; and Beckwith having only one bayonet regiment, and four companies of Riflemen, was advancing against more than twelve thousand infantry supported by cavalry and artillery. Scarcely had the

Riflemen reached the top of the hill, when a compact and strong body of French drove them back upon the 43rd.

The weather cleared at that instant, and Beckwith at once saw and felt all his danger; but, well supported as he was, it was met with a heart that nothing could shake. Leading a fierce charge, he beat back the enemy, and the summit of the hill was attained; but at the same moment two French guns opened with grape, at the distance of a hundred yards: a fresh body appeared in front, and considerable forces fell upon either flank of the regiment.

Fortunately, Reynier, little expecting to be attacked, had, for the convenience of water, placed his principal masses in the low ground, behind the height on which the action commenced; his renewed attack was therefore uphill; yet the musketry, heavy from the beginning, now increased to a storm.

The French mounted, the acclivity with great clamour; and it was evident that nothing but the most desperate fighting could save the regiment from destruction.

Captain Hopkins, commanding a flank company of the 43rd, immediately ran out to the right, and with admirable presence of mind seized a small eminence close to the French guns and commanding the ascent by which the French troops were approaching. His first fire was so sharp that the assailants were thrown into confusion: they rallied, and were again confounded by the volleys of this company: a third time they endeavoured to form an attack, when Hopkins, with a sudden charge, increased the disorder; and at the same moment the two battalions of the 52nd regiment, which had been attracted by the fire, entered the line. Meantime the centre and left of the 43rd were furiously engaged, and excited beyond all former precedent. Beckwith, wounded in the head, and with the blood streaming down his face, rode amongst the foremost of the skirmishers, directing all with ability, and praising the men in a loud, cheerful tone.

I was close to him at the time. One of our company called

out, "Old Sydney is wounded." Beckwith heard the remark, and instantly replied, "But he wont leave you: fight on, my brave fellows; we shall beat them." The musket bullets flew thicker and closer every instant; but the French fell fast: a second charge cleared the hill, a howitzer was taken, and the British skirmishers were even advanced a short way down the hill, when small bodies of French cavalry came galloping in from all parts, and obliged them to take refuge in the main body of the regiment.

Having brought down a Frenchman by a random shot, I advanced close to the poor fellow as he lay on his side. Never shall I forget the alarm that was pictured on his countenance: he thought I was going to bayonet him, to avert which he held out his knapsack, containing most likely all his worldly substance, by way of appeasing my wrath. Unwilling to injure a fallen foe, I did not take his life, and in a few seconds he was protected by a charge of cavalry.

The English line was now formed behind a stone wall above; yet one squadron of Dragoons surmounted the ascent, and with incredible desperation, riding up to this wall, were in the act of firing over it with their pistols, when a rolling volley laid nearly the whole of them prostrate. By this time, however, a second and stronger column of infantry had rushed up the face of the hill, endeavouring to break in and retake the howitzer, which was on the edge of the descent, and only fifty yards from the wall. But no man could reach it and live, so deadly was the 43rd's fire.

One of my comrades, having previously passed the howitzer, took a piece of chalk from his pocket, and, as he said, marked it as our own, and we were determined to keep it.

Reynier, convinced at last, that he had acted unskilfully in sending up his troops in small parties, put all his reserves, amounting to nearly six thousand infantry, with artillery, and cavalry into motion, and outflanking the division on the left, appeared resolved to storm the contested position.

At this critical period the 5th division passed the bridge of Sabugal, the British cavalry appeared on the hills beyond the enemy's left, and General Colville with the leading brigade of the 3rd division, issued out of the woods on Reynier's right, and opened a fire on the flank that directly decided the fate of the day.

The loss of the allies in this sanguinary contest, which did not last quite an hour, was nearly two hundred killed and wounded: that of the enemy was enormous,—three hundred dead bodies were heaped together on the hill, the greater part round the captured howitzer; and more than twelve hundred were wounded—so unwisely had Reynier managed his masses, and so true and constant was the English fire. Lord Wellington afterwards observed that this was one of the most glorious actions that British troops ever sustained. If by this term we are to understand that a numerous and well-disciplined force was signally repulsed by one of numerical inferiority, and that on the British side our national honour was upheld, he was right. In any other sense, the glories of war are, I am afraid, of a cast rather ambiguous.

I scarcely ever before saw such determined firmness in our troops. It amounted almost to invincibility. During the action there was through our ranks to be observed a fierce and terrible anger, before the breakings forth of which the enemy quailed and fled. Our fire was given with singular exactness and rapidity. This fine conduct arose partly from a sense of extreme personal danger—for of that not a man was insensible; and partly from the desire which I believe pervaded every breast, of properly supporting the officers engaged. Among others, I had been unusually excited, and had dealt out wounds and destruction with an unsparing hand. In endeavouring to reach the enemy, all concern for my own preservation was forgotten.

Just as the action commenced, a round shot struck a horseman close to my side, and brought him down. Daniel

Lowry, an intimate friend, who was also within a few paces, was slain. My old Captain was hit and badly wounded: his place was, however, well supplied by Lieutenant Brown, who succeeded in the command of the company. After the action had ceased, the latter officer was pleased to take special notice of my conduct, and by his recommendation I was made Corporal in one of the companies of the regiment.

We halted on the field of battle during the succeeding day; some of our men were quartered in a chapel which had been recently occupied by French troops. Nearly the whole of the interior fittings were destroyed. As the place had been used for Roman Catholic worship, saints and images, attired in fanciful vestments, "black, white, and grey, with all their trumpery," had been abundant. These petty divinities, despite of their alleged virtues, were upset and destroyed: some were prostrate on the floor; others were broken and disfigured; not a few had been consumed; and all that remained of many were a few glowing embers.

As food now became dreadfully scarce, a small party, of which I was one, went in search of bread or any other article of sustenance we could procure. After wandering at least ten or twelve miles from the camp ground, we observed a young heifer, to which we immediately gave chase; but the animal was so timid, and withal so swift of foot, that after a weary pursuit the game was lost.

The French soldiers had, in fact, laid waste the land. Having spread themselves over the surface of many a league, they had, like a devastating army of locusts, devoured every particle of food within reach; and what in some respects is worse, what they did not eat was destroyed.

On ascending an eminence, we saw the smoke of several burning villages. One of the men discovered also, at a moderate distance, what appeared to be two or three huts; we accordingly made for them: on arriving near the spot, we found they were tents, pitched apparently for temporary use.

Two or three women and some children presently appeared, when we asked if they had any bread and wine to sell; telling them at the same time, to secure their favour, that we were English soldiers. They were inexorable and declared they had nothing: but one of our party, not disposed to credit the ladies, forced his way into the tent, and dragged out a leathern bottle, containing perhaps twenty or thirty gallons of liquid. We flattered ourselves it was wine, but on inspection it was filled with oil. Several loaves of bread were, however, discovered, with which we made free; but had nearly paid a high price for the liberty taken.

All of a sudden the whole party of women and children set up a dismal piercing shout, and almost at the same instant a numerous and armed party of men were observed rapidly coming down the mountain-side upon us. We were few in number, and unfortunately were without our muskets. Sensible that if overtaken, our lives were forfeited, a hasty retreat became necessary. We were chased for several miles; but owing to our superior speed, we at length left our pursuers behind. When out of the reach of danger, we halted, almost dead with fatigue, and divided our spoil. It amounted to a small piece of bread for each; but how sweet that morsel was, no man can tell but he who has been driven to desperate acts by the call of biting hunger.

The next day our division took the route of Valdespina, to look out for the enemy on the side of the passes leading upon Coria; but Massena was in full retreat for Ciudad Rodrigo; and on the 5th he crossed the frontier of Portugal; so that Lord Wellington now stood victorious on the confines of that kingdom, having executed, what to others had appeared incredible and vain.

CHAPTER 25

Fuentes D'Onoro

The pursuit was continued. When Massena reached the Agueda, his cavalry detachments, heavy artillery, and convalescents, again augmented his army to more than fifty thousand men; but the fatigue of the retreat, and want of provisions, would not suffer him to show a front to the allies: he therefore fell back to Salamanca and Lord Wellington invested Almeida. Our division occupied Gallegos and Espeja, and the rest of the army were disposed in villages on both sides of the Coa.

Here Colonel Waters, who had been taken near Belmonte, rejoined the army. His escape was most extraordinary. Confident in his own resources, he had refused his parole; but when carried to Ciudad Rodrigo, he rashly mentioned his intention to the Spaniard in whose house he was lodged. This man betrayed him; but a servant, detesting his master's treachery, secretly offered his aid, and Waters coolly allowed him to get the rowels of his spurs sharpened.

When the French army was near Salamanca, Waters, being in the custody of Gendarmes, waited until their chief, who rode the only good horse in the party, had alighted; then, giving the spur to his own beast, he galloped off. This was an act of astonishing resolution and hardihood; for he was on a large plain, and before him, and for miles behind, the road was covered with the French columns. His hat fell off, and thus distinguished, he rode along the flank of the troops, some encouraging him, others firing at him, and the Gendarmes, sword in hand, close at his heels; but suddenly breaking at full speed between two columns, he gained a wooded hollow, and having baffled his pursuers, evaded the rear of the enemy's army.

The beautiful village of Fuentes d'Onoro was now destined to suffer. It had escaped all injury during the previous warfare, though occupied alternately for above a year by both sides. Every family in it was known to our division; and it was therefore a subject of deep regret to find that the preceding troops had pillaged it, leaving only the shells of houses where, three days before, a friendly population had been living in comfort. This wanton act was so warmly felt by the whole army, that eight thousand dollars were afterwards collected by general subscription for the poor inhabitants; yet the injury sunk deeper than the remedy.

The allies occupied a fine table-land, lying between the Turones and the Dos-Casos; the left at Fort-Conception, the centre towards the village of Alameda, the right at Fuentes d'Onoro, the whole distance being five miles. The first and third divisions were concentrated on a gentle declivity, about a cannon-shot behind Fuentes d'Onoro, where the line of ground occupied by the army turned back, and ended on the Turones.

The French came up in three columns abreast. General Loison fell upon Fuentes d'Onoro, which was occupied by five battalions of chosen troops. Most of the houses in this village were at the bottom of the ravine; but an old chapel, and some buildings on a craggy eminence, overhung one end. The low parts were vigorously defended; yet the violence of the attack was so great, and the cannonade so heavy, that the British abandoned the streets, and could scarcely maintain the upper ground; and the fight was becoming perilous, when three fresh regiments, coming down from the main position, charged with so little ceremony, that the French were forced back, and, after a severe contest, finally driven over the stream of Dos-Casos.

On the 4th Massena arrived; and, having examined all the line, made dispositions for the next day. Forty thousand infantry, and five thousand horse, with thirty pieces of artillery, were under arms; and they had shown, in the action of the 3rd, that their courage was not abated.

The position of the English was, on the other hand, not at all desirable; and it required no common resolution to receive battle on ground so dangerous. The action began by severe cavalry fighting; and the British horsemen, being over matched, retired behind the light division, which threw itself into squares; but the main body of the French were upon the seventh division, before the like formation could be effected: nevertheless the troops stood firm, and, although some were cut down, the Chasseurs Britanniques, taking advantage of a loose wall, received the attack with such a fire, that the enemy recoiled.

Immediately after this, a commotion was observed among the French squadrons: men and officers closed in confusion towards one point, where a thick dust was arising, and where loud cries, and the sparkling of blades, and the flashing of pistols, indicated some, extraordinary occurrence. Suddenly the multitude was violently agitated; an English shout arose, the mass was rent asunder, and Norman Ramsey burst forth at the head of his battery, his horses on full stretch, and his guns bounding along like things of no weight, with the mounted gunners in close and compact order protecting the rear. But while this brilliant action was passing in one part, the enemy were making progress in the wood, and it was evident that the battle would soon be lost if the original position was not immediately regained.

In this posture of affairs, Lord Wellington directed the seventh division to cross the Turones and move down the left bank to Frenada. General Crauford, who had resumed the command the light division, first covered the passage of the seventh, an then retired slowly over the plain in squares, having the British cavalry principally on the right flank. He was followed by the enemy's horse, which continually out-flanked him, and near the wood surprised and sabred an advanced post of the Guards, making Colonel Hill and four-teen men prisoners.

Several times Montbrun seemed disposed to storm the light division squares, but we were too formidable to be med-dled with: yet, on the authority of Colonel Napier, there was not during the war a more dangerous hour than this for Eng-land. The whole of that vast plain, as far as the Turones, was covered with a confused multitude, amidst which the squares appeared but as specks. The seventh division was separated from the army by the Turones; five thousand French cavalry, with fifteen pieces of artillery, were close at hand, impatient to charge; the infantry of the eighth corps was in order of battle behind the horsemen; the wood was filled with the skirmish-ers of the sixth corps; and, if the latter body had issued forth, our division was in imminent danger of being broken.

No effort of the sort was made: Montbrun's horsemen merely hovered about our squares; the plain was soon cleared, the cavalry took post behind the centre, and the light divi-sion formed a reserve, sending the Riflemen among the rocks to connect it with the seventh. At sight of this new front, so deeply lined with troops, the French stopped short, and com-menced a heavy cannonade, which did great execution from the closeness of the allied masses; but twelve British guns re-plied with vigour, and the violence of the hostile fire abated.

All this time a fierce battle was raging at Fuentes d'Onoro. Massena had directed Drouet to carry this village, at the very moment when Montbrun's cavalry should turn the right wing: it was, however, two hours later when the attack be-gan. The three British regiments made a desperate resist-

141

ance, but, overpowered by numbers, they were pierced and divided; two companies of the 79th were taken, Colonel Cameron was mortally wounded, and the lower part of the town was carried: the upper part was, however, stiffly held, and the rolling of musketry was incessant.

In this manner the fight lasted till the evening, when the lower part of the town was abandoned by both parties; the British maintaining the crags, and the French retiring a cannon-shot from the stream. Fifteen hundred men and officers; of which three hundred were prisoners, comprised the loss of the allies: that of the enemy was computed at five thousand, but this I have reason to believe was an exaggerated statement.

The night after the action, I was stationed on the line of-sentinels, not far from the French front, and at the extreme verge of our own: this service, which demands perpetual vigilance, requires also, on account of its wearisome and continued toil, no ordinary degree of physical energy, as the safety of the army itself often depends upon the caution and alertness with which the outposts are preserved.

Often when pacing some doubtful position, at dead of night, I have applied my ear to the ground, to try if by that means a distant footstep could be heard. At the precise time to which I now refer, the feeble voice of many a poor wounded fellow, calling for help, might be heard: these were, however, removed by the parties on both sides without delay, after which the dead were buried with as much decency and respect as circumstances allowed. A pile of about one hundred and thirty dead bodies, of which one-third were British, was discovered on a small space at Fuentes d'Onoro; and several large excavations or graves were formed, in which the remains of our fallen friends were deposited.

Soon after this period the French were compelled to evacuate Almeida; but by a singular and ingenious train of operations, the men who defended it contrived to effect their escape. During the battle of Fuentes d'Onoro, General Brennier, the Governor of Almeida, with his garrison of fifteen hundred, skirmished boldly with the blockading force, and loud explosions, supposed to be signals of communication with the relieving army, were frequently heard. When all hope of succour vanished, a soldier, named Tillet, contrived with extraordinary courage and presence of mind to penetrate, although in uniform, through the posts of the blockade, carrying Brennier's orders to evacuate the fortress.

The blockade it would appear, was imperfectly maintained: this was noticed by Brennier, who prepared to force his way through the encircling troops. An open country and a double line of troops greatly enhanced the difficulty; yet Brennier was resolved not only to cut his own passage, but to render the fortress useless to the allies To effect this, he ruined all the principal bastions, and kept up a constant fire of his artillery, so directed that the mouth of one piece crossed that of another; while therefore some shots flew towards the besiegers, and a loud explosion was heard, others destroyed pieces without attracting notice. At midnight, on the 10th, all being ready, he sprung his mines, sallied forth in a compact column, broke through the piquets, and passed between the quarters of the reserves, with a nicety that proved at once his talent of observation, and his coolness.

General Pack followed, with a few men collected at the instant, and plied him with a constant fire; yet nothing could shake or retard his column, which in silence, and without returning a shot, gained the rough country upon Barba del Puerco. Here it halted for a moment, just as daylight broke: and Pack, who was at hand, hearing that some English Dragoons were in a village, sent an officer to bring them out, thus occasioning a slight skirmish, and consequent delay. The troops of the blockade had paid little attention at first to the explosion of the mines, thinking them a repetition of Brennier's previous practice; but Pack's fire having aroused them, the 36th regiment was close at hand; and the 4th also, having heard the firing at Valde-Mula, was rapidly gaining the right flank of the enemy. Brennier, having driven off the cavalry, was again in march; yet the British regiments, having thrown off their knapsacks, followed at such a pace that they overtook the rear of his column in the act of descending the deep chasm of Barba del Puerco, killed and wounded many, captured about three hundred, and even passed the bridge in pursuit. Lord Wellington, it is said, was stung by this event, and issued a remonstrance to the army, couched in terms which no one could misunderstand.

CHAPTER 26

Albuera

When Marmont had thus recovered the garrison of Almeida, he withdrew the greater part of his army to Salamanca. Lord Wellington also set out for that province; but before he could arrive, a great and bloody battle had closed the operations. Beresford held a conference with the Spanish Generals at Valverde, on the 13th, when it was resolved to abide the enemy's attack at Albuera.

The position taken by the allied forces was, it is said, singularly defective. It was occupied by thirty thousand infantry, above two thousand cavalry, and thirty-eight pieces of artillery; but the brigade of the fourth division being still absent, the British infantry, the pith and strength of the battle, did not amount to seven thousand.

The French had fifty guns, and above four thousand veteran cavalry, but only nineteen thousand chosen infantry; yet being of one nation, obedient to one discipline, and animated by one spirit, their excellent composition amply compensated for inferiority of numbers: beside which, it is acknowledged by military men, that the talents of their General were immeasurably greater than those of his adversary.

Soult examined Beresford's position without hindrance on the evening of the 15th, and having detected the weaknesses of the entire arrangement, resolved to attack the next morning. Passing by the varied evolutions which preceded the contest, it may be sufficient to observe, that a little before nine in the morning, Godinet's division issued from the woods in one heavy column of attack, preceded by ten guns. He was flanked by the light cavalry, and followed by Werle's division of reserve; and, making straight towards the bridge, commenced a sharp cannonade, attempting to force the passage.

The allies' guns, on the rising ground above the village, answered the fire of the French, and ploughed through their columns, which were crowding without judgement towards the bridge, although the stream was fordable above and below. Beresford, convinced that the principal effort would be on the right, sent Blake orders to form a part of the first, and all the second, line of the Spanish army on the broad part of the hills, at right angles to their actual front.

Soon after, the enemy's columns began to appear on the right; and Blake, moving at last, proceeded in the evolution with such pedantic slowness, that Beresford, impatient of his folly, took the direction in person. Great was the confusion and delay thus occasioned; and before the troops could be put in order, the French were among them. In one short half hour Beresford's situation was rendered nearly desperate. Two thirds of the French were in compact order of battle, on a line perpendicular to his right, and his army, disordered, and composed of different nations, was still in the difficult act of changing its front.

The Spaniards were already in disorder; some had given way; and Soult, thinking that the whole army was yielding, pushed forward his columns, while his reserves also mounted the hill, and all the batteries were placed in position.

At this critical moment General Stewart arrived with Colonel Colborne's brigade, which formed the head of the second division. The Colonel seeing the confusion above, desired to form in order of battle previous to mounting the ascent; but Stewart, carried away by the impetuosity, of his feelings, led up without any delay in column of companies and attempted to open out his line in succession as the battalions arrived at the summit. Being under a destructive fire, the foremost charged to gain room, but a heavy rain prevented any object from being distinctly seen; and four regiments of Hussars and Lancers, which had passed the right flank in obscurity, came galloping in; upon the rear of the line, at the instant of its development and slew or took two-thirds of the brigade.

In the tumult, a Lancer fell upon Beresford; but the Marshal, a man of great strength, putting his spear aside, cast him from his saddle; and a shift of wind blowing aside the mist and smoke, the mischief was perceived from the plains by General Lumley, who sent four squadrons out upon the Lancers, and cut many of them off.

During this unhappy effort of the second division, so great was the confusion that the Spanish line continued to fire, although the British were before them; on which Beresford, finding his exhortations to advance fruitless, seized an Ensign, and bore him and his colours by main force to the front: yet the troops would not follow, and the man went back again on being released.

At this juncture, Sir William Stewart once more advanced: and the weather having cleared, he poured a dreadful fire into the thickest of the French columns, convincing Soult, that whatever might be the result, the day was not yet won. Houghton's regiments soon got footing on the summit; Dickson placed the artillery in line; the remaining brigade of the second division came up on the left; and two Spanish corps at last moved forward. The enemy's infantry then recoiled; yet soon recovering, renewed the fight with greater violence than before. The cannon on both side discharged showers of grape at half range, and the peals of musketry were incessant, and often within pistol-shot. But the close formation of the French embarrassed their battle, and the British line would not yield them one inch of ground, nor a moment of time, to open their ranks: their fighting was, however, fierce and dangerous. Stewart was twice hurt; Colonel Duckworth of the 48th was slain; and the valiant Houghton, who had received many wounds without shrinking, fell, and died in the act of encouraging his men.

Still the combat raged with unabated fury. Colonel Inglis, twenty-two officers, and more than four hundred men, out of five hundred and seventy that had ascended the hill, fell in the 57th alone: and the other regiments were much the same in loss; not one-third were standing in any. Ammunition failed; and as the English fire slackened, the enemy established a column in advance upon the right flank the play of Dickson's artillery checked them for a moment, but again the Polish Lancers charged, and captured six guns. In this desperate crisis, Colonel Hardinge boldly ordered Cole to advance; and then riding to Colonel Abercrombie, who commanded the remaining brigade of the second division, directed him also to push forward into the fight.

The die being thus cast, the terrible battle was continued. The field was heaped with carcasses; the Lancers were riding furiously about the captured artillery on the upper slope of the hill; and on the lower parts a Spanish and an English regiment, in mutual error, were exchanging volleys; behind all, some Portuguese, in withdrawing from the heights above the bridge, appeared to be in retreat. All now appeared to be lost, when all was in a few minutes gained, by the conduct of a few brave and unconquerable men. Colonel Arbuthnot pushing between the fire of the mistaken troops, enlightened their minds; while Cole, with the Fusiliers, flanked by a battalion of the Lusitanian legion, mounted the hill, dispersed the Lancers, recovered the captured guns, and soon appeared on the right of Houghton's brigade.

Such a gallant line, issuing from the midst of the smoke, and rapidly separating itself from the confused and broken multitude, startled the enemy's heavy masses, which were increasing and pressing onwards as to an assured victory: they wavered, hesitated, and then vomiting forth a storm of fire, hastily endeavoured to enlarge their front, while a fearful discharge of grape from a their artillery whistled through the British ranks.

Myers was killed Cole, and the three Colonels, Ellis, Blakeny, and Hawkshawe, fell wounded; and the Fusilier battalions, struck by the iron tempest began to reel. In that moment, when the last particle of energy appeared to be gone, they arose in almost unprecedented might, and surpassed their former selves. Closing at once with their enemies, the strength and intrepidity of a British soldier were exhibited in deeds seldom seen.

In vain did Soult, by voice and gesture, animate his Frenchmen; in vain did the hardiest veterans, extricating them selves from the crowded columns, sacrifice their lives to gain time for the mass to open out, on so fair a field; in vain did the mass itself bear up, and, fiercely striving, fire indiscriminately upon friends and foes, while the horsemen, hovering on the flank, threatened to charge the advancing line. Nothing could stop that astonishing infantry: their eyes were bent on the dark columns in front; their firm, heavy, and measured tread shook the ground; their dreadful volleys swept away the head of every formation; their deafening shouts overpowered the dissonant cries that broke from all parts of the tumultuous crowd, as foot by foot, and with horrid carnage, it was driven by the vigour of the attack to the extreme edge of the hill. Here the last stand was made, with the hope of averting this mountain torrent. But it was in vain: the effort only served to increase the irremediable confusion; and the mighty mass giving way, like a loosened cliff, went headlong down the ascent.

The rain flowed after in streams discoloured with blood; and of six thousand British soldiers who performed these wonders, fifteen hundred unwounded men were all that remained upon the fatal hill. The serious fighting had endured only four hours; and in that space of time nearly seven thousand of the allies, and above eight thousand of their antagonists, were struck down. Three French Generals were wounded, two slain, and eight hundred soldiers so badly hurt as to be left on the field.

On Beresford's side, beside the loss of the British already named, two thousand Spaniards, and six hundred Germans and Portuguese, were killed or wounded. The trophies of the French were five hundred unwounded prisoners, a howitzer, and several stand of colours: the British had nothing of that sort to display; but the piles of carcasses within their lines told, with convincing eloquence, who were the conquerors; and all the night the rain poured down, and the rivers, and hills, and woods resounded with the groans of dying men. On the 18th Soult retreated.

Chapter 27

Ciudad Rodrigo Assaulted

Towards winter I was charged with a mission to fetch clothing from Lisbon for the use of the regiment. One description of article was flannel shirts, of which I received six hundred, for the approaching winter wear.

On returning, I met with an accident, which had nearly deprived me of sight. One of our party, with consummate carelessness, placed his powder-horn upon the table, fully charged, and by some accident the whole quantity exploded: my face was sadly scorched, but providentially the organs of vision received no lasting injury. On returning with the property for the army, I found my way into considerable trouble. Our party consisted of six or seven persons: of these, three were Corporals; and of these three I was senior, and therefore sustained the responsibility of every act.

Having to pass over several mountains of vast height, our progress was necessarily slow. One evening, having ascended the slope of a stupendous hill, on which the snow was deep, we were unable to move the cars on which the stores were carried. Having also but an imperfect knowledge of the pass, we found ourselves compelled to spend the night in that bleak and desolate region. All the shelter we could procure was to creep under the cars. Two of the men, were soon after seized with ague, and suffered extremely. The silence which prevailed in this elevated region was singularly impressive.

After a wearisome night, which appeared almost endless, we were happy to perceive the first morning ray. We soon after discovered a man coming our way, driving two bullocks: I thought the omen a happy one; and in the spirit of the national war then raging I ordered the man to stop, and without hesitation pressed the animals into our service, by yoking them to our cars. The driver demanded my authority for so doing: I told him to look at my musket.

To my dismay I afterwards found that some of the troops had been in the habit of laying violent hands upon cattle, having no other object in view than to extort money from the owners when they applied to reclaim their property. To put down this practice, Lord Wellington had issued a proclamation, which, unfortunately, I had not heard, denouncing these excess in terms of great severity. In fact, strange as it appeared to myself who had no intention of violating general orders, on my arrival at quarters, I was handed over to the Provost-Marshal, deprived my arms and accoutrements, and thrown into confinement among some of the most ill-favoured vagabonds that ever infested man beast. The officer in whose custody I was placed, proved himself one of Job's comforters. He gave me to understand, that not long since a man in the 52nd had been shot for the exact crime of which I was guilty: he then closed the prison-door and departed Conscious, however, that I had intended neither to rob nor injure my mind was supported. I was released as if nothing had happened.

After my enlargement had taken place, I found that my worthy comrades had been to the owner of the animals, and had exhausted the entire circle of a soldier's pleading on my behalf. I was young; had not heard of the late order; knew no better; used no violence; asked for no money; was an Irishman: beside which they gave him to under stand that I was a good Catholic; to which I believe they subjoined a little cash in hand: these two latter arguments were irresistible, and the matter was smoothly settled.

The new year opened with uncommon effort on the side of the British forces in Spain. Lord Wellington, whose means of collecting information were extensive and correct, had discovered that a considerable reduction had taken place in the French army. The Imperial Guards, seventeen thousand strong, were required for the Russian war, and had returned to France; so that the force in the Peninsula was diminished by sixty thousand men. Marmont was also deceived, by what appeared to him the careless winter attitude of the allies, and Ciudad Rodrigo was left unprotected. The Frenchman was mistaken; and Wellington resolved to show that he was, by grasping at that fortress.

The troops disposable for the attack of Ciudad Rodrigo were about thirty-five thousand, Including cavalry. From the scarcity of transports, only thirty-right guns could be brought to the trenches, and these would have wanted their proper supply of ammunition, if eight thousand shot had not been found among the ruins of Almeida. When the place was closely examined, it was found that the French, in addition to the old works, had fortified two convents. They had also constructed an enclosed and pallisadoed redoubt upon the greater Teson; and this redoubt, called Francisco, was supported by two guns and a howitzer, placed upon the flat roof of the convent of that name.

On minutely inspecting these enlarged works, it was resolved to storm Fort Francisco, and, opening the first parallel along the greater Teson, to form counter-batteries, with which to ruin the defences, and drive the besieged from the convent.

Meanwhile, to cover the siege, Julian Sanchez, and Carlos d'Espana, were posted in observation of the enemy.

On the 8th of January, the eighth division and some Portuguese forded the Agueda near Caridad, three miles above the fortress, and making a circuit took post beyond the great Teson. As there was no regular investment, the enemy did not believe that the siege was commenced; but in the evening the troops stood to their arms, and Colonel Colborne, commanding the 52nd, having assembled two companies from each of the British regiments of the light division, stormed the redoubt of Francisco: of this party I had the honour to make one.

The attack was so rapid and furious that the assailants appeared to be at one and the same time in the ditch, mounting the parapets, fighting on the top of the rampart, and forcing the gorge of the redoubt, where the explosion of one of the French shells had burst the gate open. The post was taken with the loss only of twenty-four men and officers; and working parties were set to labour on the right of it, for the fort itself was instantly covered with shot and shells from the town.

This tempest continued through the night; but at daybreak the parallel, six hundred yards in length, was sunk three feet deep, and four wide: the communication over the Teson to the rear was completed, and the progress of the siege was hastened several days by this well-managed assault.

I was exposed to the fire of the enemy for some time previous to our arrival at the fort, but sustained no injury. We were discovered when about a hundred and fifty yards from the fort. After the redoubt had been taken, I was employed with several others escorting the prisoners to a place of safety. The garrison, it seems, had no expectation of this unceremonious visit; and when we entered the place I observed several packs of cards, with which the men had been amusing themselves.

On returning, I unexpectedly came in contact with a French soldier, who by some means other had escaped notice. I called out instantly, desiring him to surrender, which he did; but while in the act of conducting him to the others, a British Sergeant, who deserves to be named, but on whom compassionate silence shall be shown, stopped the prisoner for the sake of plunder. Enraged at this unjust and discreditable interference, I placed my gun on the ground, determined to knock down the interloper, and secure my captive. A scuffle accordingly ensued; when, in an instant, we found, to our dismay, that further contention was needless. The Frenchman, observing our quarrel, instantly took to his heels, and, being exceedingly alert, was out of sight before I could fire at him.

On the 12th we were employed in the trenches, from whence we picked off the enemy's gunners. The Riflemen also, taking advantage of a thick fog, did great execution; but in the night the weather was so cold, and the besieged shot so briskly, that little progress was made.

Two days afterwards, the enemy, having observed that the men in the trenches went off in a disorderly manner on the approach of the relief, made a sally, and overturned the gabions of the sap; they even penetrated to the; parallel, and were upon the point of entering the batteries, when a few of the workmen getting together, checked them until a support arrived, and thus the guns were saved. This affair, together with the death of the engineer on duty, and the heavy fire from the town, delayed the opening of the breaching batteries; but at half-past four in the evening, twenty-five heavy guns battered the rampart and two pieces were directed against the convent of Francisco. The spectacle was sublime.

The enemy replied by more than fifty pieces; the bellowing of eighty large guns shook the ground far and wide; the smoke rested in heavy columns upon the battlements of the place; the walls crashed to the blow of the bullet; and when night put an end to this turmoil! the quick clatter of musketry was heard like the pattering of hail after a peal of thunder; for the 40th regiment assaulted and carried the convent of Francisco, and established itself on the suburb on the left of the attack.

On the 17th the firing on both side was very heavy, and

the wall of the place was beaten down in large cantles; but several of the besiegers' guns were dismounted, their batteries injured, and many of their men killed.

General Borthwick, the Commandant of the artillery, was wounded, and the sap was entirely ruined. Even the Riflemen in the pits were at first overpowered with grape; yet towards evening they recovered the upper hand, and the French could fire only from the more distant embrasures. In the night the battery intended for the lesser breach was armed, and that on the lower Teson raised, so as to afford cover in the day-time. On the 10th it was reported that both breaches were practicable, and a plan of attack was immediately formed.

All the troops reached their different posts without seeming to attract the attention of the enemy; but be fore the signal was given, and while Lord Wellington was still at the convent of Francisco, the attack on the right commenced, and was instantly taken up along the whole line. The space between the army and the ditch was then ravaged by a tempest of grape from the ramparts.

The storming parties of the third division jumped out of the parallel when the first shout arose; but so rapid had been the movements on their right, that before they could reach the ditch, three regiments had already scoured the *fausse-braye*, and were pushing up the great breach, amid the bursting of shells, the whistling of grape and muskets, and the shrill cries of the French, who were driven fighting behind the retrenchments. There, however, they rallied, and, aided by the musketry from the houses, made hard battle for their post; none would go back on either side, and yet the British could not get forward; and men and officers, filling in heaps, choked up the passage, which was incessantly raked with grape from two guns flanking the top of the breach at the distance of a few yards.

It was now our turn. We had three hundred yards to clear; but, impatient of delay, we did not wait for the hay-bags, but swiftly ran to the crest of the glacis, jumped down the scarp a depth of eleven feet, and rushed up the *fausse braye*, under smashing discharge of grape and musketry. The bottom of the ditch was dark and intricate, and the forlorn hope took too much to their left; but the storming party went straight to the breach, which was so contracted, that a gun placed lengthwise across the top nearly blocked up the opening. Here the forlorn hope rejoined the stormers; but when two-thirds of the ascent were gained, the leading men, crushed together by the narrowness of the place,; staggered under the weight of the enemy's fire.

Our Commander, Major Napier, was at this moment struck to the earth by a grape-shot, which shattered his arm, but he called on his men to trust to their bayonets; and all the officers simultaneously sprang to the front, when the charge was renewed with a furious shout, and the entrance was gained. The supporting regiments then came up in sections abreast, and the place was won. During the contest, which lasted only for a few minutes after the *fausse-braye* was passed, the fighting had continued at the great breach with unabated violence; but when the 43rd, and the stormers of the light division, came pouring down on the right flank of the French, the latter yielded to the storm; at the same moment the explosion of three wall-magazines destroyed many persons, and the third division with a mighty effort broke through the retrenchments.

The garrison fought for a short time in the streets, but finally fled to the castle, where an officer, who, though wounded, had been amongst the foremost at the lesser breach, received the Governor's sword. The allies now plunged into the streets from all quarters; after which, throwing off the restraints of discipline, frightful excesses were committed. The town was fired in three or four places; the soldiers menaced their officers, and shot each other; many were killed in the marketplace; intoxication soon increased the disorder; and at last, the fury rising to an absolute madness, a fire was wilfully lighted in the middle of the great magazine, when the town, and all in it, would have been blown to atoms, but for the energetic courage of some officers and a few soldiers, who still preserved their senses.

Three hundred French had fallen; fifteen hundred were made prisoners; and beside the immense store of ammunition, above one hundred and fifty pieces of artillery were captured in the place. The whole loss of the allies was about twelve hundred soldiers, and ninety officers; and of these above six hundred and fifty men, and sixty officers, had been slain or hurt in the breaches. General Crauford and General Mackinnon were killed. With these died many gallant men; and amongst others, a Captain in the regiment to which I belonged. Of him it was felicitously said, that "three Generals and seventy other officers had fallen; but the soldiers fresh from the strife only talked of Hardyman."

Unhappily, the slaughter did not end with the battle; for the next day, as the prisoners and their escort were marching out by the breach, an accidental explosion took place, and numbers of both were blown into the air. The personal sufferings of the soldiers were severe, as the service had been unusually dangerous.

While in the front ditch near the glacis, a live shell exploded within a few paces of the spot on which I stood: we threw ourselves flat on the ground, but, though nearly suffocated by the dust it threw around, no material injury was inflicted either on myself or comrades. The station I was ordered to take on the following day was of a melancholy cast. It was in the ditch, among the unburied dead.

Nothing struck me more forcibly than the conduct of a soldier's widow. Suspecting that her husband had fallen, she traversed this vale of death to seek him. Never shall I forget the anguish of her soul when she discovered the much-loved remains. The brave man had fallen covered with wounds. His countenance was sadly disfigured, and suffused with blood. She fell upon his face, and kissed his faded lips. She then gazed at the lifeless form, repeated her embraces, and gave way to the wild and ungovernable grief which struggled for expression. Sin! what hast thou done? Nor can I forbear observing, that a noble disregard for suffering, and fortitude of no common kind, were frequently shown both by officers and men, those severely hurt and disabled. None retired to the rear, until compelled by stern necessity.

This resolute disposition to surmount, and if possible forget, all surmountable difficulties, reminds me of a French royalist officer, in the late revolutionary war. Being engaged in a desperate action, he had the misfortune to have both his legs carried away by a cannon-ball. While lying on the ground, a wounded soldier indulged in loud and clamorous complaints: "Peace, friend," said the officer: "our God died upon the cross; our King perished on the scaffold; and I have lost my limbs. Revere the Almighty, and be patient."

The siege of Ciudad Rodrigo lasted twelve days. When the Commander-in-chief terminated his order for the assault, with this sentence, "Ciudad Rodrigo must be stormed this evening," he knew well that it would be nobly understood. The difficulties we had to encounter were great. The principal breach was cut off from the town by a perpendicular descent of six teen feet; and the bottom was planted with sharp spikes, and strewed with live shells. The houses behind were all loop-holed and sprinkled with musketeers.

The French had left their temporary bridges, but behind were parapets so powerfully defended, that it was said the third division could never have carried them, had hot the light division taken the enemy in flank. To recompense an exploit so boldly undertaken and so nobly finished, Lord Wellington was created Duke of Ciudad Rodrigo, by the Spaniards, Earl of Wellington, by the English, and Marquis of Torres Vedras, by the Portuguese.

CHAPTER 28
Badajos

Soon after the close of the siege just described, I received, in conjunction with others who were similarly entitled, my share of prize-money, on account of the property captured some years before at Copenhagen. Some arrears of pay were also supplied by the hands of Major Wells. A little good advice was kindly subjoined. We were exhorted to save our money, to avoid excesses, and spend with economy. But alas! how hardly shall they that are rich keep in the path of moderation and humility. The cash burnt m our pockets. The intimations so civilly given were altogether wasted, and might as well have been addressed to our knapsacks. No sooner did opportunity offer, than the wine-houses washed away, not only all our good advices, but the whole of our hard-earned pittance so recently distributed. When a man is determined to indulge in liquor, he is almost sure to find some justification for it. It is commonly of Dean Aldrich's sort, more wordy than wise:

Good wine, old friends, or being dry,
Or that he may be by and by,
Or any other reason why.

I am sorry to admit that I was carried away with the torrent of sensuality, which at this time set in with a kind of powerful flood-tide.

160

It has been observed by an acute military writer, that the talents of Lord Wellington rose with his difficulties; and notwithstanding the serious impediments which obstructed the measure, he resolved to subdue the important fortress of Badajos.

He accordingly proceeded to Elvas, which he reached on the 11th of March, and arrangements were immediately commenced for the formal investment of the place. Badajos is a regularly fortified town. The garrison, composed of French, Hessian, and Spanish troops, was now near five thousand strong. Phillipon, the Governor, had greatly improved the defences of the place. A second ditch had been dug at the bottom of the great one, which was also in some parts filled with water. The gorge of the Pardaleras was inclosed, and that outwork was connected with the body of the place, from whence powerful batteries looked into it. The three western fronts were mined; and on the east, the arch of the bridge behind the San Roque was built up to form an inundation two hundred yards wide, which greatly contracted the space by which the place could be approached by troops; and all the inhabitants had been compelled, on pain of being sent away, to lay up food for three months.

The plan fixed upon by the besiegers was, to attack the bastion of Trinidad, because the counter-guard there being unfinished, the bastion could be battered from the hill on which Picurina stood. Of nine hundred gunners present, three hundred were British, the rest Portuguese; and there were one hundred and fifty sappers, volunteers from the third division.

In the night of the 17th eighteen hundred men broke ground one hundred and sixty yards from the Picurina. A tempest, which happened to arise, stifled the sound of their pickaxes; and though the work was commenced late, a communication four thousand feet in length was formed, and a parallel of six hundred yards, three feet deep, and three feet six inches wide, was opened. However, when the day broke, the Picurina was reinforced; and a sharp musketry, interspersed with discharges from some field-pieces, aided by heavy guns from the body of the place, was directed on the trenches. On the 19th Lord Wellington, having secret intelligence that a sally was intended, ordered the guards to be reinforced. Nevertheless, at one o'clock, some cavalry came out by the Talavera gate; and thirteen hundred infantry, under the command of General Vielland, filed unobserved into the communication between the Picurina and the San Roque. These troops, jumping out, at once drove the workmen before them, and began to demolish the parallel.

Previous to this outbreak the French cavalry, forming two parties, had commenced a sham-fight on the right of the parallel; and the smaller party, pretending to fly, and answering Portuguese to the challenge of the piquets, were allowed to pass. Elated by the success of their stratagem, they then galloped to the engineers' park, which was a thousand yards in the rear of the trenches, and there cut down some men,—not many, for succour soon came; and meanwhile the troops at the parallel, having rallied upon the relief which had just arrived, beat the enemy's infantry back, even into the castle.

In this hot fight the besieged lost above three hundred men and officers, the besiegers only one hundred and fifty; but Colonel Fletcher, the chief engineer, was badly wounded; and several hundred trenching-tools were carried off;—for Phillipon had promised a high price for each: yet this turned out ill; for the soldiers, instead of pursuing briskly, dispersed to gather the tools. After the action, a squadron of Dragoons, and six field-pieces, were placed as a reserve-guard behind St. Michael and a signal-post was established on the Sierra de Venta, to give notice of the enemy's motions.

On the 24th the fifth division invested the place, on the right bank of the Guadiana: the weather was fine, and the batteries were heavily armed.

The next day at eleven o'clock, the pieces opened but were so vigorously opposed, that one howitzer was dismounted, and several artillery and engineer officers were killed. Nevertheless, the San Roche was silenced; and the garrison of the Picurina was so galled by the marksmen in the trenches, that no man dared look over the parapet. Hence, as the external appearance of the fort did not indicate much strength, General Kempt was charged to assault it in the night. The outward seeming of the Picurina was, however, fallacious: the fort was very strong; the fronts were well covered by the glacis; the flanks were deep; and the rampart, fourteen feet perpendicular from the bottom of the ditch, was guarded with thick slanting pales above; and from thence to the top there were sixteen feet of an earthen slope.

Seven guns were mounted on the works, the entrance to which, by the rear, was protected with three rows of thick paling; the garrison was above two hundred strong, and every man had two muskets. The top of the rampart was furnished with loaded shells, to pushover; and finally some small mines, and a loop-holed gallery under the counter scarp intended to take the assailants in rear, were begun, but not finished.

Five hundred men of the third division being assembled for the attack, General Kempt ordered two hundred, under Major Rudd, to turn the fort on the left; an equal force, under Major Shaw, to turn the fort by the right; and one hundred from each of these bodies were directed to enter the communication with San Roche, and intercept any succours coming from the town. The engineers, with twenty-four sappers bearing hatchets and ladders, guided these columns; and fifty men of the light division, provided also with axes, were to move out of the trenches at the moment of attack.

The night was fine, the arrangements clearly and skilfully made, and about nine o'clock the two flanking bodies moved forward. The distance was short, and the troops quickly closed on the fort, which, black and silent before, now seemed one mass of fire: then the assailants, running up to the palisades in the rear, endeavoured to break through; and when the destructive musketry of the French and the thickness of the pales rendered their efforts useless, they turned against the faces of the work, and strove to break in there; but the depth of the ditch, and the slanting stakes at the top of the brick-work, baffled them.

At this time, the enemy firing incessantly and dangerously, the crisis appeared imminent; and Kempt sent the reserve headlong against the front: thus the fight was continued strongly; the carnage became terrible; and a battalion coming out from the town to succour the fort, was encountered, and beaten by the party on the communication.

The guns of Badajos and of the castle now opened; the guard of the trenches replied with musketry; rockets were thrown up by the besieged; and the shrill sound of alarm-bells, mixing with the shouts of the combatants, increased the tumult. Still Picurina sent out streams of fire, by the light of which dark figures were seen furiously struggling on the ramparts; for Powis first escaladed the place in front, where the artillery had beaten down the pales; and the other assailants had thrown their ladders on the flanks, in the manner of bridges, from the brink of the ditch to the slanting stakes; and all were fighting hand to hand with the enemy. Meanwhile the axe-men of the light division, compassing the fort like prowling wolves, discovered the gate, and hewing it down, broke in by the rear.

Yet the struggle continued: Powis, Holloway, Gips and Oats, of the 88th, fell wounded in or beyond the rampart. Nixon, of the 52nd, was shot, two yards within the gate; Shaw, Rudd, and nearly all the other officers, had fallen outside: and it was not until nearly half the garrison were killed, that Gasper Thiery, the Commandant, and eighty-six men surrendered, while a few rushing out of the gate endeavoured to cross the bridge, and were drowned. This intrepid assault, which lasted an hour, cost four officers and fifty men killed, fifteen officers and two hundred and fifty men wounded; and so vehement was the fight throughout, that the garrison either forgot or had not time to roll over the shells and combustibles arranged on the rampart.

On the 3rd of April it was evident that the crisis of the siege drew nigh. The British guns being all turned against the curtain, the masonry crumbled rapidly away; in two hours a yawning breach appeared; and Lord Wellington, having examined the points of attack in person, gave the order for assault. The soldiers then made themselves ready for the approaching combat, one of the most fierce and terrible ever exhibited in the annals of war. Posterity will find it difficult to credit the tale, but many who are still alive know that it is true. The British General was so sensible of Phillipon's firmness, and of the courage of his garrison, that he spared them the affront of a summons; yet, seeing the breach strongly entrenched, and the enemy's flank fire still powerful, he would not in this dread crisis trust his fortune to a single effort. Eighteen thousand soldiers burned for the signal of attack, and as he was unwilling to lose the services of any, to each division he gave a task such as few Generals would have the hardihood to contemplate. Nor were the enemy idle, for while it was yet twilight some French cavalry issued from the Pardaleras, escorting an officer, who endeavoured to look into the trenches, with a view to ascertain if an assault was intended; but the piquet on that side jumped up, and, firing as it ran, drove him and his escort back into the works. The darkness then fell, and the troops awaited the signal.

With respect to myself, I could not help largely sharing in the general desire to advance: indeed, our duty in the trenches had been so severe, that, in spite of approaching peril, we had no objection to move. I had been stationed in battery number six, and was frequently exposed to a terrific raking fire from the besieged.

Directions, I remember, were given on one occasion to fill a quantity of sand-bags. Poor Woollams, a private in the regiment, and myself, worked together; he held the mouth of the sack open, while I threw in the sand with a shovel: before we had been long thus engaged, a shell struck his knee, and in an instant severed his leg, which dropt on the ground: he fell backwards, while the shell, which lodged in the earth at a few feet distance, had burnt nearly to the exploding point. Aware of the approaching danger, I threw myself on my face; and I had scarcely taken the precaution when the shell burst with ruinous effect. Stones, dust, and fragments of timber were scattered in all directions; and among other substances whirled into the air, was the lost limb of my comrade. I knew it while descending by the pattern of the gaiter. As the leg was useless, I ran to the sufferer to whom it had belonged, tied my coat-strap round his thigh to check the effusion of blood, and, after placing him in a blanket, carried him to the nearest hospital, where surgical assistance was promptly afforded.

On my return to the trenches, another friend was borne off greatly hurt: a comrade was loading his musket, and while the ramrod was in the barrel, the piece was accidentally discharged. The ramrod pierced through his body, and so firmly was the worm-end fixed near the backbone, that the strongest man among us was unable to move it. He was conveyed to the infirmary, and things went on as usual, as no calamity of this sort could be allowed to interfere with the duties then before us. The fine young man, whose case is just recorded, recovered from the wound, but was, I believe, eventually drowned in a river near Salamanca.

At another time, during a violent cannonade from the besieged, I had been conversing with a man on the trenches, when our discussion was closed by a round shot, which took away the head of the respondent, as smoothly as if it had been sabred. I was also informed that another of our men had been killed merely by the wind of a cannon-bullet; but as I did not witness the circumstance, I will not vouch for its correctness.

Not long before the storming parties were selected, a sad in one of the fatal effects of intemperance occurred. One of our company was ordered out on duty, but, being in a state of inebriety, durst not appear. We afterwards missed him altogether; and some time after, we found his lifeless body coiled up in a blanket, in a crouching posture, behind one of the tents. Our opinion was, that he had crept there for secrecy, and by some means or other was smothered. All that remained in our power we did, which was to consign his remains to the parent earth.

The day on which we proceeded to Badajos I received a letter from my brother in Ireland, in which he recommended me to an officer named Carey. After some search I found the gentleman, who received me with genuine kindness, and promised his future patronage when the town was taken; an engagement on which, from his frank and generous bearing, I at once felt it was safe to depend. But, Lord, what is man, or the best of men? My newly-acquired friend fell while leading on his men; so that our brief intercourse was the first and last which this world afforded.

We were now selected and classified for the actual assault. The difficulty was, not to procure men enough, but how to refuse applications,—for all were ready. Nor were these offers founded in ignorance of the nature of the expected service: the candidates were not such novices. The watchword of Nelson was not forgotten—"England expects every man to do his duty;" and the resolution which everywhere prevailed, was entered into with a thorough consciousness that life was then scarcely worth an hour's purchase. And yet every countenance was bright, for every heart was firm; and it was clear that the elevation and strength of mind so universally prevalent, was the effect of principle, well considered, and approved. Indeed, there was no stimulus at hand, to produce superficial excitement; no drops of Scheidam, to generate Dutch courage: the men were kept in the utmost silence and order. It is true, here and there a soldier might be perceived stealing from the trenches, with a little refreshment in his canteen for the friend with whom he was to part; and in return, more than one message, the last to be delivered on earth, was sent from many a brave man to mother, wife, or some other valued relative, with directions that if killed, the knapsack of a certain number, with its contents, should be duly forwarded.

The night was dry, but clouded; the air thick with watery exhalations from the river; the ramparts and the trenches were unusually still, yet a low murmur pervaded the latter, and in the former, lights were seen to flit here and there; while the deep voices of the sentinels at times proclaimed that all was well in Badajos. The French, confiding in Phillipon's direful skill, watched from their lofty station the approach of en-emies, whom they had twice before baffled, and now hoped to drive a third time, blasted and mined, from the walls.

At ten o'clock the whole of the works were to have been simultaneously assailed, and it was hoped that the strength of the enemy would shrivel before this fiery girdle; but the disappointments of war are many. An unforeseen accident delayed the attack of the 5th division; and a lighted carcass thrown from the castle falling close to where the men of the 3rd division were drawn up, discovered their array, and obliged them to anticipate the signal by half an hour.

Then, everything being suddenly disturbed, the dou-ble columns of the 4th and light divisions also moved si-lently and swiftly against the breaches; and the guard of the trenches rushing forward with a shout, encompassed the San Roque with fire, and broke in so violently that scarcely any resistance was made.

General Kempt passed the Rivellas in single files by a

narrow bridge, under a terrible musketry; and then reforming and running up the rugged hill, had reached the foot of the castle, when he fell severely wounded, and being carried back to the trenches, met Picton, who hastened forward to take the command.

Meanwhile his troops spreading along the front reared their ladders, some against the lofty castle, some against the adjoining front on the left, and with incredible courage ascended amidst showers of heavy stones, logs of wood, and bursting shells rolled off the parapet; while from the flanks the enemy plied his musketry with fearful rapidity, and in front with pikes and bayonets stabbing the leading assailants, or pushed the ladders from the walls; and all this attended with deafening shouts, and the crash of breaking ladders, and the shriek of soldiers crushed by violent falls. Still, swarming round the remaining ladders, these undaunted veterans strove who should first climb; until all being overturned, the French shouted victory, and the British, baffled but untamed, fell back a few paces, and took shelter under the rugged edge of the hill.

Here, when the broken ranks were somewhat reformed, the heroic Colonel Ridge, springing forward, called with stentorian voice on his men to follow; and seizing a ladder, once more raised it against the castle, yet to the right of the former attack, where the wall was lower, and an embrasure offered some facility. A second ladder was soon placed alongside the first, by the Grenadier officer Canch; and the next instant he and Ridge were on the rampart: the shouting troops pressed after them; the garrison, amazed, and in a manner surprised, were driven fighting through the double gate into the town, and the castle was won. A reinforcement sent from the French reserve then came up a sharp action followed, both sides fired through the gate, and the enemy retired; but Ridge fell,—and no man died that night with greater honour.

During these events, the tumult at the breaches was such, as if the very earth had been rent asunder, and its central fires were bursting up uncontrolled. The two divisions had reached the glacis in silence; as yet no stir was heard, and darkness covered the breaches. Some hay-packs were then thrown, several ladders placed, and the forlorn hopes and storming parties of the light division, about five hundred in all, had descended into the ditch without opposition, when a bright flame shooting upwards displayed all the terror of the scene. The ramparts, crowded with dark figures, and glittering arms, were on the one side; and on the other the red columns of the British, deep and broad, were coming on like streams of burning lava. A crash immediately followed, and the storming parties were dashed to pieces with incredible violence by the explosion of hundreds of shells and powder barrels.

The place which fell to my lot was just in the centre of this hurly-burly. With what similitude to illustrate our condition at that moment, I know not. The regular discharge of musketry at given distances, and the usual clash of arms, in field-warfare, is rather rough, to say the least of it; but the collision of hostile forces in open space, where the combatants may evade approaching ruin, is civil pastime compared with this deadly ditch-conflict. Each of the men fought as if the issue of the assault depended on his single arm. As to timidity, the thing was unknown: every drum-boy acted well. Shielded by Eternal Mercy, all undeserving as I was, my life was preserved. Not that it then appeared even to myself worth consideration. All thought of self-protection was banished from the corps in general. Every nerve and muscle was strained to the utmost tension in the struggle; among the whole body there appeared to be only one heart; and in the attempt to reach the ramparts all other considerations merged. But what an assemblage of furies; the excitement was indescribable.

Fancying that the man immediately behind myself did

not press forward with sufficient energy, I turned round, and with imprecations of which the bare remembrance causes regret, I declared that if he did not push on I would shoot him. Most likely I was wrong, not only in language but in opinion: I have since thought the man did his best; but in the raging of such a tempest, mistakes were easily made, and the mere notion of defective effort ignited the passions. For one instant we stood on the brink of the ditch, amazed at the terrific sight; then with a shout that matched even the sound of the explosion, the men flew down the ladders, or, disdaining their aid, leaped, unmindful of the depth, into the gulf below.

The fourth division came running after, and followed with like fury: there were, how ever, only five ladders for both columns, which were close together; and a deep cut made in the bottom of the ditch as far as the counter-guard of the Trinidad, was filled with water from the inundation; into this watery snare the head of the fourth division fell, and it is said that above a hundred of the Fusiliers, the men of Albuera, were there smothered.

Great was the confusion at this juncture; for now the ravlin was crowded with men of both divisions, and while some continued to fire, others ran down and jumped towards the breach; many also passed between the ravlin and the counter-guard of the Trinidad; the two divisions got mingled; and the reserves, who should have remained at the quarries, also came pouring in, until the ditch was quite filled,—the rear still crowding forward, and all cheering vehemently. The enemy's shouts were also loud and terrible; and the bursting of shells and of grenades, the roaring of the guns from the flanks, answered by the iron howitzers from the battery of the parallel, the heavy rolls and explosion of the powder-barrels, the flight of the blazing splinters, the loud exhortations of the officers, and the continued clatter of the muskets, made a maddening din.

Impatient of delay, a heavy column now bounded up the great breach; but across the top glittered a range of sword-blades, sharp-pointed, keen-edged on both sides, and firmly fixed in ponderous beams, which were chained together and set deep in the ruins; and for ten feet in front the ascent was covered with loose planks studded with sharp iron points, on which the feet of the foremost being set, the planks moved, and the unhappy soldiers, falling forward on the spikes, rolled down upon the ranks behind. Then the French men, exulting at the success of their stratagem, and leaping forward, plied their shot with terrible rapidity; for every man had several muskets, and each musket, in addition to its ordinary charge, contained a small cylinder of wood, stuck full of leaden slugs, which scattered like hail when they were discharged.

At the beginning of this dreadful conflict, Colonel Andrew Barnard had, with prodigious efforts, separated his division from the other, and preserved some degree of military array: but now the tumult was such that no command could be heard distinctly, except by those close at hand; and the mutilated bodies, heaped on each other, and the wounded, struggling to avoid being trampled upon, broke the formations. Order was unattainable: yet officers of all stations, followed more or less numerously by the men, were seen to start out, as if struck by sudden madness, and rush into the breach.

In one of these attempts, Colonel McLeod, of our regiment, a young man, whose feeble body would have been quite unfit for war, had it not been sustained by an unconquerable spirit, was killed. Wherever his voice was heard, there his soldiers gathered; and with such a strong resolution did he lead them up the fatal ruins, that when one behind him in falling plunged a bayonet in his back, he complained not, and, continuing his course, was shot dead within a yard of the sword-blades. Two hours spent in these , vain efforts convinced the soldiers that the breach of the Trinidad was impregnable. Gathering in dark groups, and leaning on their muskets, they looked up with sullen desperation; while the enemy, stepping out on the ramparts, and aiming their shots by the light of the fire-balls which they threw over, asked, as their victims fell, "why they did not come into Badajos!"

About midnight, when two thousand brave men had fallen, Wellington, who was on a height close to the quarries, sent orders for the remainder to retire, and re-form for a second assault; for he had just then heard that the castle was taken, and, thinking the enemy would still hold out in the town, was resolved to assail the breaches again. This retreat from the ditch, however, was not effected without further carnage and confusion; for the French fire never slackened, and a cry arose that the French were making a sally from the distant flanks, which caused a rush towards the ladders. Then the groans and lamentations of the wounded, who could not move, and expected to be slain, increased; many officers, who had not heard of the order, endeavoured to stop the soldiers from going back, and so would even have removed the ladders, but were unable to break through the crowd.

All this time, the third division was lying close to the castle; and, either from the fear of risking the loss of a point which ensured the capture of the place, or that the egress was too difficult, made no attempt to drive away the enemy from the breaches. On the other side, however, the fifth division had commenced the false attack on the Pardaleras; and on the right of the Guadiana, the Portuguese were sharply engaged at the bridge. Thus the town was begirt; for General Walker's brigade, having pressed on during the feint on the Pardaleras, was escalading the distant bastion of San Vincente. His troops had advanced along the banks of the river, and reached the French guard-house at the barrier gate undiscovered, for the ripple of the waters smothered the sound of their footsteps; but just then the explosion at the breaches took place, the moon shone out, and the French sentinels, discovering the columns, fired. The British troops, immediately springing forward under a sharp cover of musketry, began to hew down the wooden barrier at the covered way, while the Portuguese, being panic-stricken, threw down the scaling-ladders. Nevertheless, the others snatched them up again, and forcing the barrier, jumped into the ditch; but the guiding engineer officer was killed; and when the foremost man succeeded in reaching the ladders, the latter were found too short, for the walls were generally above thirty feet high.

Meanwhile the fire of the French was deadly, a small mine was sprung beneath the soldiers' feet, beams of wood and live shells were rolled over on their heads, showers of grape from the flank swept the ditch, and man after man dropped dead from the ladders. Fortunately, some of the defenders having been called away to aid in recovering the castle, the ramparts were not entirely manned; and the assailants, having discovered a corner of the bastion where the scarp was only twenty feet high, placed three ladders there, under an embrasure which had no gun, and was only stopped with a gabion. Some men with extreme difficulty got up, for the ladders were still too short; and the first man who gained the top was pushed up by his comrades, and then drew others after him, until many had gained the summit; and though the French shot heavily against them from both flanks, and from a house in front, they thickened and could not be driven back.

Half the 4th regiment entered the town itself to dislodge the enemy from the houses while the others pushed forward towards the breach, and by dint of hard fighting successively mastered three bastions. In this disorder a French reserve, under General Viellande, drove on the British advance with a firm and rapid charge, and pitching some men over the walls, and killing others outright, again cleared the ramparts even to the San Vincente.

There, however, Colonel Nugent had taken his station with a battalion of the 38th, as a reserve; and when the French came up, shouting and slaying all before them, this battalion, about two hundred strong, arose, and with one close volley destroyed them. The panic then ceased; the soldiers rallied, and in compact order once more charged along the walls towards the breaches; but the French, although turned on both flanks, did not yield.

Meanwhile the detachment of the 4th regiment, which had entered the town when the San Vincente was first carried, was strangely situated; for the streets were empty, and brilliantly illuminated, and no person was seen; yet a low murmur or whisper was occasionally heard, lattices were now and then gently opened, and from time to time shots were fired from underneath the doors of the houses. However, the troops, with bugles sounding, advanced towards the great square of the town; and in their progress captured several mules going with ammunition to the breaches. At length the French were beaten back, other parties entered the place; and finally, General Viellande, and Phillipon, who was wounded, seeing all ruined, passed the bridge with a few hundred soldiers, and entered San Cristoval, where they all surrendered early the next morning, upon summons, to Lord Somerset, who had with great readiness pushed through the town to the draw-bridge before they had time to organize further resistance.

CHAPTER 29

Wounded

In these protracted conflicts many of the finest soldiers in the British army met their fate, and fell in the firm and vigorous discharge of their duty. Of these, numbers might have been preserved had they chosen to have fallen back; but it was with them a point of honour to gain the breach or die on the spot. So wonderful is the resolution of a noble heart; and so much the more is it to be regretted, that power, so morally invincible, should be employed in the sad purpose of human destruction.

For my own part, my mind had been unhesitatingly made up from the first shot that was fired, that so long as life and consciousness continued, I would fulfil my commission to the best of my ability. As the battle grew hot I caught the contagion that burned all around, and in this desperate and murderous mood advanced to the breach of Trinidad. My pride perhaps wanted to be repressed; and while in the act of marching, I was wounded in the left thigh by a musket-shot, which remains unextracted to this day, and will probably go with me to the grave.

At first, not disposed to heed the casualty, I affected to despise such a trifle, and continued to fight on. Nature, however, refused her support; and after firing a few times, I felt myself getting weak and feverish. What rendered my situation worse, was, that at that precise moment the report of the unexpected sally of the French was circulated. Had that been realized, my doom would have been sealed, as I could neither resist nor retreat. In this condition, faint with loss of blood, I contrived to descend into the ditch with the help of my musket.

Meanwhile the depth of water by some added inundation had been increased, and no ladder was to be discovered for my ascent on the opposite side. Unwilling to die there, I made another effort, and at length observed a ladder standing in front of the ditch. Unable to get up with my musket, I reluctantly left that behind, and scrambled up with extreme difficulty. Numerous shots were fired at me while ascending, and I perceived bullets whistling through the rounds of the ladder, but not one of them struck me. But I was sadly grieved at the loss of my musket: it had been a faithful friend to me. I seldom knew it to fail in the hour of need: the number on it was seventy-seven.

Having succeeded in gaining the summit, I found, to my surprise, a young man belonging to the gallant Napier's company, who kindly offered his arm, and supported me to the field-hospital. He was amongst the bravest where all were brave, and, though unhurt, had stood in the fore-front and pinnacle at the severest point of strife. With so large an influx of patients, it will be supposed that the hospital attentions were not very prompt: I was placed on the ground, with many others in a worse condition than myself, to await my turn for surgical assistance. After some hours I found that unless my wound ceased bleeding I should not long survive: this, with a little contrivance, I managed to effect. But the most intolerable sensation was that of raging thirst: all my worldly substance, ten times valued, would have been no price at all for a draught of water.

Meantime the frost was so severe, that my limbs appeared to be deprived of flexibility and motion. In the course of the night, hearing a deep moan at a little distance, I called out, "Who is there?" and was answered:

"It's me, Tom."

The voice was familiar, and I found it was that of Patrick Murphy, an old comrade and countryman, in Dalzell's company, who had fought most nobly through several campaigns. He had been miserably burnt while endeavouring to force the breach, and suffered extremely.

In the course of a day or two we were placed in military spring wagons, and conveyed to Elvas. We were after wards transferred to bullock-carts: a mode of conveyance not remarkable either for comfort or speed; the carriages were clumsily constructed, and ensured very little in the way of easy riding; added to which, we moved only at the rate of about one mile an hour.

I have to add with sorrow that the conquest of Badajos was attended with excesses that tend to tarnish the soldier's character. All, indeed, were not alike, for hundreds risked and many lost their lives in striving to stop the violence; but the madness of ungovernable licentiousness generally prevailed and as the worst men were leaders here, all the dreadful passions of human nature were displayed: shameless rapacity, brutal intemperance, savage lust, cruelty and murder, shrieks and piteous lamentations, groans, shouts, curses, the hissing of fires bursting from the houses, the crashing of doors and windows, and the reports of muskets used in violence, re-sounded for two days and nights in the devoted town.

Five thousand men and officers fell during the siege; and of these, including seven hundred Portuguese, three thousand five hundred had been stricken in the assault,—sixty officers and more than seven hundred men being slain on the spot. Five Generals were wounded; about six hundred men and officers fell in the escalade of San Vincente, as many at the castle, and more than two thousand at the breaches,—each division there losing about twelve hundred.

Let any man picture to himself this frightful carnage taking place in a space of less than a hundred square yards. Let him consider that the slain died not all suddenly, nor by one manner of death; that some perished by steel, some by shot, some by water, that some were crushed and mangled by heavy weights, some trampled upon, some dashed to atoms by fiery explosions; that for hours this destruction was endured without shrinking; and that the town was won at last;—let any man consider this, and he must admit that a British army is by no means deficient either in physical or moral excellence.

And it would be unjust to withhold the need of praise from the French; the garrison stood and fought manfully and with good discipline, behaving worthily. Some of the instances of personal valour on each side were wondrous.

A soldier of the 95th, in his resolution to win, thrust himself beneath the chained sword-blades, and there suffered the enemy to dash his head in pieces with the ends of their muskets; and the foremost man who entered the Santa Maria was an intrepid Portuguese Grenadier, who was killed on the spot. Ferguson, of the 43rd, had received two deep wounds in former assaults; and yet, though not half cured, he was here leading the stormers of his regiment, the third time a volunteer, and the third time wounded. In a former action a French officer was observed in the heat of battle in the act of striking at the gallant Felton Harvey, of the 14th Dragoons, when, on perceiving that he had only one arm, the high-minded Gaul, with a rapid movement, brought down his sword into a salute, and passed on. Traits like this are worth preservation.

On alighting from our vehicles at Elvas, we were at first placed in a dark, uncomfortable apartment, adjoining the fortifications; the roof was of arched masonry, and so damp on the inner side, that water fell on us in large drops. Our attendants were also nothing to boast of; for under pretence of bringing our haversacks containing provisions, they walked away with them altogether—an evil against which we knew no remedy, being unable, through weakness, to search for the depredators, or procure more food. The confusion in this unhappy lazar-house was extreme. Every man naturally thought his own case the most serious, and that it demanded care before all others.

We were not, however, destined to remain long in these unsuitable quarters: orders were received directing our removal to Estramores, and our journey thither was commenced the same night. The procession was rather melancholy: several times we had to halt in order to bury some poor creature, who, exhausted by suffering, had fled away.

On our arrival at Estramores, we found accommodation more suited to the exigencies of the invalided guests: a convent, sufficiently spacious, had been fitted up as a military hospital, and was well adapted for the purpose.

When able to look around, I discovered several of my former associates. Here lay the man through whose body a ramrod had forced its way. On another couch reposed Patrick Marr, a daring fellow, but of bad character. He, with others, had led on the forlorn hope, and was violently struck with a musket-bullet. Then there was a young man named Forbes, who volunteered with myself into the 43rd: in a short period he died. Having an excellent constitution, I soon recovered my health, and in the course of a few weeks was pronounced convalescent.

In the winter of 1812 I was stationed at Gallegos; and on the 13th of January, 1813, was promoted to the rank of Sergeant, in the place of one Hicks, who had recently died at Lisbon. Soon after this professional lift, one of the army physicians was desirous of inspecting such of the non-commissioned officers and men as had been wounded, or who, through length and severity of service, were supposed to require rest: among these, I was one. On entering ; the room, Surgeon Gilchriest related several particulars concerning my past experience, when my name was included in a list of men who were directed to return to England.

CHAPTER 30

Ordered to England

We then proceeded, without loss of time, to Lisbon, es-
corted by a detachment of the 95th. Mules were provided
for us as far as Abrantes, after which we proceeded by water.
I am sorry to observe, that several of our party, thus indulged,
ill requited the kindness shown, by drinking to excess; and
am sorrier still to add, that I was weak enough to swell the
number. The consequence was, that after a halt, when the
detachment was ready to proceed, we were unprepared. The
officer in command, a very young man, mildly remonstrated
with me on the impropriety of such conduct: I answered
with unbecoming rudeness; on which he drew his sword,
and I flourished my cane. Several men, wiser than myself,
then interfered, and mischief was prevented.

My opinion is that a man altogether overcome with strong
liquor is beside himself, and should be consigned to the care
of his friends, if he have any, until he is *compos mentis* and may
be safely trusted in social society. Next day I saw my error,
and made an apology for the rudeness of the preceding day.

When we had arrived to within six leagues of Lisbon, we
landed for a short time, waiting for the return of tide, leaving
in our boat a man named Latimer, in company with a Portuguese waterman. During that interval, Latimer, who was in
jesting humour, amused himself by soliciting the poor Portuguese to give him cigars. Not receiving what he expected,

he foolishly took up a musket, forgetting it was loaded, and presented the muzzle to his unfortunate companion, jocularly observing, at the same time, that if he did not give him a cigar he would shoot him. He accordingly snapped the lock, and blew out the man's brains, which, with part of his skull, were scattered about the boat.

On arriving at Lisbon, I was half afraid that the officer with whom I had taken an unwarrantable liberty might call me to serious account for the misdemeanour, especially as it had taken place so soon after my promotion, when better things were expected; but I had the happiness to find that he knew both how to forget and forgive. He was an English officer; which in every correct vocabulary means a gentleman, and no mistake. He parted with me in excellent humour, and presented me with a small pecuniary balance at that time due for arrears of pay.

Soon after my arrival at Lisbon, three soldiers were sentenced to death for desertion; and while waiting for conveyance to England, I was ordered, among others, to mount guard at the execution. One of the men, being a Roman Catholic, was attended by Priest of that community; the other two were assisted by a Protestant Clergyman. On arriving at the appointed spot, which was on the sands near Belem Castle, a party of soldiers, who were to fire at the culprits, was drawn up in front, with their pieces loaded. The sufferers were ordered to kneel at the usual distance; and in sight of all were the graves prepared for their reception. Just before the signal was given to fire, a Dragoon galloped up with a reprieve for the Roman Catholic. The man, however, was so enfeebled and overcome, that he was unable, for some time, to rise from his knees, or take the least notice of this extraordinary deliverance. The other two men were shot. Why the distinction was made, I know not; but with out doubt, there were circumstances in the conduct of each, that called for lenity in the one instance, and severity in the other two.

Our embarkation was immediately after effected; and, having put to sea, we were favoured with a brief and agreeable voyage to the Isle of Wight, at which place we landed, and marched into Albary barracks. In the month of May, 1813,I again joined the 2nd battalion of the 43rd. Nothing surprised me more than the number of new faces in the corps: such had been the ravages arising from accident, death, and other mischances of active warfare, that few only of my old associates remained, so that the regiment was to me nearly strange and new. My old ragged coat, fairly worn out, was exchanged for a new and handsome dress, ornamented with the professional insignia of my recently acquired rank; and the first time I appeared on parade with the men, was on the 4th of June, a day at that time of cheerful and loyal celebration, being the birthday of the then reigning Monarch, George the Third.

In the course of the summer, wishing to see my friends, I applied to the Colonel of the regiment for a furlough granting permission for that purpose. Leave was given; and, that the service might at the same time be promoted, I was charged with the command of a party of men who were to proceed to, and be stationed at, Castlebar, in Ireland. None but those who have visited and been detained in foreign lands, can conceive aright of the intense desire that arises in the mind, at intervals, to visit the country of their forefathers.

Breathes there a man with soul so dead,
Who never to himself hath said,
This is my own, my native land?

The supposition is incredible. Indeed, any circumstance which, while in Spain, induced me to think of Ireland, was affecting; and I well remember the emotion felt on one occasion, merely because, on commencing a march, the band struck up the national air of "Saint Patrick's day in the morning." Being directed to embark at Liverpool, I hastened there with the detachment, without delay; and having engaged passages on board the packet for Dublin, our luggage was shipped.

My evil genius once more prevailed, and was so far present, as to seduce me, and, of course, the soldiers under my direction, to enter a public house of entertainment for refreshments, which might perhaps have been dispensed with. Forgetting ourselves, which those who love the potent glass are sure to do, we remained too long, so that on walking to the pier, we discovered, to our no small dismay, that the packet had sailed. As negligence of this sort amounted to a breach of orders, I was apprehensive, in addition to the disappointment personally felt, of incurring the displeasure of my superior officer; beside which, our property was on board the vessel.

Not a moment was to be lost. I therefore engaged a boat then on the beach, told the master to name his own price, and directed him to crowd all his canvass and strive to overtake the packet. We were instantly on board and under sail, standing out to sea in the track of the departed ship. Unfortunately the wind rose considerably, which created a great swell, so that after long and wearisome exertion, we had gained but little on the packet.

We were at length perceived by the Captain, who civilly shortened sail, lay to, and received us on board. Such are the penalties to be paid for unguarded delay.

CHAPTER 31

Ireland

Next evening I was refreshed beyond measure by a sight of the Pigeon-House in the Bay of Dublin; and soon after placed my feet on Irish soil.

One whole week, which seemed to be endless, expired before I had an opportunity of seeing my relatives. At the end of that time I could no longer refrain, and made a forced march to the neighbourhood, with a heart as light and devoid of care as may be desired. Every object was delightful. There was nothing like it any where else: the shrubs were so green; the sky was so bright and blue; the air so sweet; and even the earth was more soft and verdant than in other regions of the globe.

Having to pass near the residence of a beloved sister, who, with her husband and family, occupied a farm at Philipstone, I formed a little plan, and pleased myself with it, of taking her by surprise. I accordingly walked slowly to the house, as a wandering veteran in search of lodgings. As I expected, she did not know me; and no wonder. When last in her company, I was a mere gay and laughing youth: now she saw the weather-beaten sunburnt visage of an unknown soldier, with his knapsack and side-arms, on whose countenance middle age had begun to limn a few serious lines. I began by informing her that my billet directed me to her house for quarter.

"I take no soldiers here; you cannot be received."

"But you will not be so hard as to turn me away! See how late it is."

"Perhaps it may be; but I cannot provide for the like of you."

"Surely that is not what you mean to say: some of your family are, likely enough, gone soldiering; and what would you think if either of them were served so?"

"That cannot happen. I had one brother, younger than myself, who listed in the army; but we shall never see him again: he was killed in battle."

"Indeed! Perhaps I might have known him: pray what was his name?"

"Why, if it can be of any consequence to you, it was Thomas".

"To be sure it was, sister; and here he is now. What! do you not know your brother!"

I need not describe the raptures of the interview. I kissed her; she wept for joy; explanations, inquiries, and wonderments, almost without measure or end, succeeded. In a few minutes the report of my arrival got abroad: some thought it unlikely; others were sure it was impossible, unless the dead could be raised.

Indeed, I discovered that letters had been received, stating that I had been slain at Badajos. Ocular demonstration, however, soon settled all debate; and congratulations, such as few but an Irishman yields, were tendered with true sincerity and friendship.

I proceeded without loss of time to my mother's residence. Having been misled by the report of my decease, she could scarcely credit the testimony of her senses when I appeared before her: great indeed was her exultation and my pleasure at meeting once more on earth. Nor did the time occupied by this social visit hang heavily upon my hands. Among other enterprises which attracted my notice, I made proposals of marriage to an excellent young woman, who was generous enough to listen; the preliminaries were soon arranged; we were shortly after united and to this day, I have reason to be thankful for the choice then made.

Beside all this, I had to detail my adventures to numerous groups of listeners, each of whom must have a new version of the strange man's tale. The thirst was unquenchable for notices—

Of breaches, ambuscadoes, Spanish blades,
Of healths five fathom deep;

with all the other vanities and circumstance of war. Being in high spirits, aided it is likely with a little vanity, so likely to cleave to a man who seeks to recommend himself by feats of arms I had no objection to dwell occasionally upon the perils and deliverances of bygone time. But during the whole of this season my spirit was not humbled by the least sense of moral defect. I knew nothing of myself. Indeed, such was the loftiness of carriage which I thought it right to assume, that it was with me a point of honour never to sustain an affront unavenged. And yet, on looking back, I can trace an invisible but resistless influence, which even then guided me aright, and saved me from various threatening dangers: what I mean is, I was never utterly abandoned to my own devices.

CHAPTER 32

Journey's End

My furlough having expired, I returned to England, and landed at Liverpool, in the winter of 1814; which was remarkable for one of the hardest frosts known in this country for many preceding years. Here I received orders from the Paymaster to proceed to Kent, with a party of recruits destined for that district: and as most of the young fellows were rude and unruly, and strangers to military restraint, it required no common share of firmness, tempered with discretion, properly to conduct and manage them. I arrived, without missing a man, in the vicinity of Maidstone. Just before entering the town, one of the most ungovernable of the squad contrived to dip his hands in mischief; nor was his mouth entirely guiltless. Having run up a score at one of the road-side inns, for liquors had and drunk, he was unable to pay the reckoning; when, being minus his ready cash, he proposed leaving some valuable equivalent in the hands of the landlord, as a temporary deposit, to be shortly redeemed: this consisted of a bundle, containing, he averred, much valuable property.

We had not proceeded far on our journey, when poor Boniface came running after us, stating, that on opening the package it contained nothing but a few worthless rags. Meantime the shuffler, apprehensive of detection, and no doubt conscience-stricken, had purposely out-walked us, and was considerably in advance when the plaintiff over took us. We could only pity his sad case, and preach caution for the future. The troublesome personage just adverted to was the author of more mischief.

At our next halt, under the influence, it is probable, of the late excesses, he quarrelled with the servants in the house; and being a powerful man, of about six feet two inches in height, soon cleared the public room of its inmates: getting into the street, he threw off his coat, and gave a general challenge for a fight. The invitation was properly rejected; and, like many other violent spirits, he was eventually subdued, and marched quietly to quarters.

Here I received unexpected orders to proceed to Plymouth. On my arrival there, I was stationed in the citadel. My removal was providential. I here met with an old friend, by whose side I had fought in Spain: he had received a commission as Captain in the 2nd battalion. The last time we had met was on the ramparts of Ciudad Rodrigo, where he was dreadfully scorched by an explosion of combustibles. He introduced me in a very handsome manner to several officers in the garrison, and made honourable mention of my former conduct; by his influence I was also appointed Colour-Sergeant to the company.

While at Plymouth, an order was issued which gave the soldiers liberty to attend such places of public worship as they thought fit, only it was expected that each should keep to his own community. When the order was read, I fell out for the Roman Catholic, where I continued some time to attend. The truth is, it mattered little by what name my religion was designated; for it was utterly worthless. I recollect that, one wet Sunday morning, it was my turn to march the Catholic party to Stonehouse chapel. The piety of the others was about equal to mine. Finding ourselves rather damp from the rain, it was proposed, that instead of going to mass, we should adjourn to the next public house. This was agreed to without a division; and there we remained till nightfall.

In the month of March, 1817, the second battalions of several regiments, in order to reduce them to the peace establishment, were disbanded; and that in which I served was of the number. We were inspected, previously to dismission, by the medical officer; and though my services had not extended the length required by rule, yet, in consideration of the wounds I had received, I was placed upon the pension-list for an allowance or one shilling *per diem*. Thus disengaged from the toil of military avocation, I felt desirous of directing my steps homeward again: I accordingly crossed the Channel, and arrived safely at Portarlington, Queen's County, in the month of May.

Coming events again introduced me to the army. In November, 1819, the pensioners were called up for examination, that those who were fit for service might be enrolled as a veteran battalion. For that purpose I went to Carlow, and was deemed by the inspector fit for the duty required. After continuing there several weeks, directions were received, ordering that the whole of the Sergeants, excepting four or five, should be dispensed with. The matter was decided among us by lot, and the decision happened to be against me. As I was placed by this event in disadvantageous circumstances, and excluded from the rank to which I felt myself entitled, I at once enlisted in the 7th Foot, intending to serve my full period of time, and be thus ultimately entitled to an increased pension.

With this view I resolved to conduct myself with strict propriety. But what are human resolutions? Can the Ethiop change his skin, or the leopard her spots? Just as soon can man reform himself, independently of divine principles. Without descending to particulars, I relapsed into conviviality and habitual dissipation. Strong drink ruined all my existing prospects. There were several religious men in the regiment, who expostulated with me on the folly of such conduct; but such were my ignorance and depravity, their words were as an idle tale. Nor, in fact, was I in other respects at home in the regiment. I missed the partners of my former dangers and hard service, men who not only talked of war, but had turned the tide of battle. We had also certain interests in which we seemed to be proprietors in common; and now I felt myself comparatively alone, and among strangers. New friends are like new wine: when it is old, it drinks better.

We lay for some time at Newcastle, and from thence removed to Tynemouth Castle: while at the latter place, I was the means, under Providence, of saving the life of a fellow-creature. During a heavy gale of wind, a sloop was driven ashore near the barracks, and all hands on board were in danger of perishing. The waves broke frightfully over the deck, sweeping in their course every moveable, and threatening quick destruction to the ship. The crew clung to the rigging with trembling and uncertain grasp. Hundreds of spectators lined the shore; but though all felt deep concern, none knew how to assist.

At last a rope was by some means conveyed from the vessel to the beach, and soon after hauled tight: a young sailor and myself then ventured on it, through the surf, and reached the vessel in safety. Among others, the Captain threw himself overboard, but missed his hold of the rope, and sank. He was under water some time, when I dived in search of him, and having fortunately grasped him by the hair, was able to raise his head above the surface of the water. The next moment we were both struck by a powerful wave, which sent us with rapidity on the shelving rocks, where we were picked up by several persons who came to assist. I was much exhausted for several hours, but in the evening was sufficiently recovered to walk to the inn, and inquire for the Captain's welfare. He had been carefully attended, and, though much bruised, was doing well. He knew me at the first glance, and exclaimed, "That's the man that saved my life. I hope the country will reward him." Several gentlemen, frequenting the Library and

Reading-room, who saw the occurrence, were equally loud in their praises; and a Clergyman, I understood, moved that I be rewarded with ten pounds and a silver medal. For distinctions so flattering I ought perhaps to be grateful; for they are all the reward I ever had.

Why the worthy Captain should expect the country to produce a premium for the saving of his life, I am at a loss to conjecture. One would have thought that the onus of doing that might have been laid upon a party much easier of access. Never from that time did I hear from these eloquently grateful parties.

In November, 1823, on another reduction in the army, I finally retired from the service.

Chapter 33

Encomiums

I have wandered over sea and land; have been in perils both of flood and field; in "hair-breadth 'scapes" I have rivalled Othello's self; for several years I was dangerously familiar with the bayonet-point and whistling bullet; and have followed a profession whose element is strife and bloodshed. While thousands have fallen, I am preserved in the land and light of the living; and, what is perhaps an equal mercy, am placed in a situation in which I have become conscious of these obligations, and where the privileges of church-fellowship exist in rich abundance. It would be ungrateful, also, were I not to acknowledge the uncommon kindness with which several of the officers under whom I served furnished me, on application, with testimonials relative to my previous conduct in the army.

It would be mere affectation were I to profess myself indifferent to opinions so generously expressed; and as military reputation, founded on faithful services, is frequently the only riches of which an old soldier can boast, I shall be pardoned for introducing some extracts from letters received about this time from several gentlemen well known in superior military circles. I ought to premise, that I had applied to Lieut. Col. Williamson, Commandant at the Royal Military Asylum, Chelsea, for admission into that institution as one of the superintendents of the children; to secure which, I found it necessary to obtain respectable references as to previous character. Colonel Pearson observed concerning me:

> I have much pleasure in stating, that his conduct on every occasion merited my most perfect approbation, and that I consider him highly qualified for any situation which requires activity, sobriety, and integrity; and as such I beg leave to recommend him.

Major Page, under whose notice I had acted at Tynemouth, certified that he had known me for several years, during which period he was pleased to say, that my conduct as a soldier gave great satisfaction; and, With reference to an event in my life already alluded to, adds,

> .... he particularly distinguished himself, and was the means of rescuing from a watery grave three or four sailors. I recollect his plunging through the surf and bringing a sailor on shore, at the time no boat would quit the beach. I cannot say too much in this soldier's praise; and nothing gives me greater pleasure than to recommend him.

To make assurance doubly sure, Colonel Napier added, that I had served in the 43rd regiment nearly eleven years; had been at the reduction of Copenhagen in 1807; at General Moore's retreat to Corunna in 1808, and the following year; and at the battles of Almeida, Busaco, Pomhal, Condeixa, Sabugal, Fuentes d'Onore, Ciudad Rodrigo, and Badajos, at which latter place he was severely wounded in the head and thigh.

These nails, driven so forcibly, to fasten my respectability, were clenched by Lieutenant-Colonel Puffy, who also spoke of me in very handsome and obliging terms. Captain Patteson then advanced, by stating concerning me:

> I had every reason to be satisfied with his steady, sober, honest, and soldier-like conduct, and had frequent op-

portunities of observing his brave and valiant behaviour in the field.

Besides these, which told heavily on the Board, I had a letter of similar import from Lieutenant-Colonel Booth, who was condescending enough to bring up the reserve, and enclose his recommendatory note in another written and directed to myself, in which he remarks,

I have great pleasure in stating what I remember of your character in the 43rd regiment, for I have a perfect remembrance of you; and it is gratifying to myself that you remember your old corps with so great affection. You are entitled to our best wishes, as one of those good and gallant soldiers who contributed to support the reputation of the regiment during the Peninsular war.

I have been induced to quote these flattering notices, not for the purpose of self-esteem, and finding food for vanity;—for, after all, I only did my duty; and for that, no one that I know of, whether in the army or elsewhere, is entitled to any extraordinary gratulations;—but I am anxious to show, that alertness and vigilance are neither unnoticed nor unrewarded in the British army; and that the superior officers are not unwilling to recollect an old and wounded soldier, when the recognition can assist him. Supported by such respectable rank and influence, my efforts to gain admission into the Asylum were successful, and in the month of December, 1823, I was received as a Company Sergeant.

ALSO FROM LEONAUR

AVAILABLE IN SOFTCOVER OR HARDCOVER WITH DUST JACKET

THE JENA CAMPAIGN: 1806 *by F. N. Maude*—The Twin Battles of Jena & Auerstadt Between Napoleon's French and the Prussian Army.

PRIVATE O'NEIL *by Charles O'Neil*—The recollections of an Irish Rogue of H. M. 28th Regt.—The Slashers— during the Peninsula & Waterloo campaigns of the Napoleonic wars.

ROYAL HIGHLANDER *by James Anton*—A soldier of H.M 42nd (Royal) Highlanders during the Peninsular, South of France & Waterloo Campaigns of the Napoleonic Wars.

CAPTAIN BLAZE *by Elzéar Blaze*—Elzéar Blaze recounts his life and experiences in Napoleon's army in a well written, articulate and companionable style.

LEJEUNE VOLUME 1 *by Louis-François Lejeune*—The Napoleonic Wars through the Experiences of an Officer on Berthier's Staff.

LEJEUNE VOLUME 2 *by Louis-François Lejeune*—The Napoleonic Wars through the Experiences of an Officer on Berthier's Staff.

FUSILIER COOPER *by John S. Cooper*—Experiences in the 7th (Royal) Fusiliers During the Peninsular Campaign of the Napoleonic Wars and the American Campaign to New Orleans.

CAPTAIN COIGNET *by Jean-Roch Coignet*—A Soldier of Napoleon's Imperial Guard from the Italian Campaign to Russia and Waterloo.

FIGHTING NAPOLEON'S EMPIRE *by Joseph Anderson*—The Campaigns of a British Infantryman in Italy, Egypt, the Peninsular & the West Indies During the Napoleonic Wars.

CHASSEUR BARRES *by Jean-Baptiste Barres*—The experiences of a French Infantryman of the Imperial Guard at Austerlitz, Jena, Eylau, Friedland, in the Peninsular, Lutzen, Bautzen, Zinnwald and Hanau during the Napoleonic Wars.

MARINES TO 95TH (RIFLES) *by Thomas Fernyhough*—The military experiences of Robert Fernyhough during the Napoleonic Wars.

HUSSAR ROCCA *by Albert Jean Michel de Rocca*—A French cavalry officer's experiences of the Napoleonic Wars and his views on the Peninsular Campaigns against the Spanish, British And Guerilla Armies.

SERGEANT BOURGOGNE *by Adrien Bourgogne*—With Napoleon's Imperial Guard in the Russian Campaign and on the Retreat from Moscow 1812 - 13.